# WORSHIP RESOURCES OF
# THE UNITED METHODIST
# HYMNAL

# WORSHIP RESOURCES OF
# THE UNITED METHODIST
# HYMNAL

## Hoyt L. Hickman

### Volume Editor

ABINGDON PRESS
NASHVILLE

WORSHIP RESOURCES OF THE UNITED METHODIST HYMNAL

Copyright © 1989 by Abingdon Press

*This book is printed on acid-free paper.*

**Library of Congress Cataloging-in-Publication Data**

Hickman, Hoyt L.
    Worship resources of the United Methodist hymnal / Hoyt L.
Hickman.
       p.   cm.
    Bibliography: p.
    **ISBN 0-687-43150-6 (alk. paper)**
    1. United Methodist hymnal—History and criticism. 2. United
Methodist Church (U.S.)—Liturgy. 3. Methodist Church—Liturgy.
I. Title.
BX8337.H53   1989
264'.076—dc20                                                            89-32532
                                                                              CIP

The prayer on page 192 has been adapted for this book by Grant S. White from the
Lucernary prayer of Hippolytus found in *Hippolytus: A Text for Students* (Grove Liturgical
Study No. 8), copyright 1976 by Geoffrey J. Cuming. Used by permission of Kenneth
Stevenson, literary executor.

Scripture quotations labeled NEB are from *The New English Bible.* © The Delegates of the
Oxford University Press and The Syndics of the Cambridge University Press 1961, 1970.
Reprinted by permission.

The service on pages 82-84 is from *A Service of Word and Table.* Copyright © 1984 by The
United Methodist Publishing House. Used by permission.

The Great Thanksgiving on pages 142-43 is from *The Book of Services.* Copyright © 1985 by
The United Methodist Publishing House. Used by permission.

The services on pages 166-68 and the service on pages 168-72 are from *The Book of Services.*
Copyright © 1985 by The United Methodist Publishing House. Used by permission.

Selections on pages 115-18 from the Psalter are from The United Methodist Liturgical
Psalter, edited by Harrell Beck, John Holbert, S T Kimbrough, Jr., and Alan Luff, © 1989
The United Methodist Publishing House, based on the New Revised Standard Version
Bible, 1989, and adapted by permission of the Division of Christian Education of the
National Council Churches of Christ in the USA, all rights reserved.

MANUFACTURED BY THE PARTHENON PRESS AT
NASHVILLE, TENNESSEE, UNITED STATES OF AMERICA

# CONTENTS

# PREFACE

This is one of a pair of books designed to help you understand and use *The United Methodist Hymnal*. The other book, *The Hymns of The United Methodist Hymnal* deals with the large middle section of the hymnal entitled "Hymns, Canticles, and Acts of Worship." This book deals with the worship resources in the front and back of the hymnal: "General Services," "Psalter," and "Other Acts of Worship."

As you pick up the hymnal and start using it, you will probably have many questions. These two books are designed to answer your questions.

This book is intended to help you use the worship resources in the hymnal. You will no doubt find some of them familiar and easy to use in your accustomed way. This book may, however, suggest to you more interesting and effective ways of using these than you have yet tried. Other worship resources will not be familiar to you. This book will help you understand their purpose, to introduce them in your local church, and use them effectively.

This volume is the work of several persons. The executive editor was Carlton R. Young, editor of *The United Methodist Hymnal*. The volume editor and principal writer was Hoyt L. Hickman, Director of Resource Development in the Section on Worship of The General Board of Discipleship. He was also editor of *Companion to the Book of Services* (Abingdon Press, 1988), from which parts of this book have been adapted. The basic writer of chapter 6 is Laurence Hull Stookey, professor of preaching and worship at Wesley Theological Seminary, writer of the Services of the Baptismal Covenant, and chair of the Worship Resources Subcommittee of the Hymnal Revision Committee. The writer of chapter 7 was Charles Michael Smith, pastor of Highland United Methodist Church of Raleigh, North Carolina, and chair of the Psalter Subcommittee of the Hymnal Revision Committee. Dwight W. Vogel, director of music at Garrett-Evangelical Theological Seminary, added to this chapter some of the directions for singing the psalms and canticles. The writer of chapter 10 was Thomas A. Langford III, assistant general secretary of the Section on Worship of The General Board of Discipleship and writer of the Orders of Daily Praise and Prayer in the hymnal.

For further information about any of the worship resources in the hymnal, write or telephone the Section on Worship, P.O. Box 840, Nashville, Tennessee 37202 (615-340-7070).

# CHAPTER 1

# THE STRUCTURE OF THE HYMNAL

## A. THE HYMNAL IS OUR BOOK OF WORSHIP

Next to the Bible, the hymnal is the primary book of United Methodist worship. This is as true for us today as it was for those who have gone before us in the Methodist, Evangelical, and United Brethren traditions. This is why our hymnals in recent generations have contained not only hymns but other worship resources as well—Psalter, Ritual, orders of worship, and acts of worship.

With this in mind, the 1984 General Conference "constituted and authorized a quadrennial Hymnal Revision Committee to prepare a single volume hymn and worship book for congregational use in The United Methodist Church and to submit the contents of this book to the 1988 General Conference for adoption as the official hymnal of The United Methodist Church."[1] The Committee faithfully followed this mandate, and the 1988 General Conference adopted *The United Methodist Hymnal: Book of United Methodist Worship* as the official hymnal of The United Methodist Church. The main title follows our long-accepted and understood practice of calling the people's book of worship the "hymnal," while the subtitle recognizes the fact that this hymnal is a comprehensive book of worship and not simply a book of hymns.

## B. THE BASIC STRUCTURE

Because the hymnal is a comprehensive book of worship, all recent Methodist and Evangelical United Brethren hymnals

---

1. *Daily Christian Advocate* of the 1984 General Conference, pages E-86, 402, 567, 610-13, 718.

have begun with one or more orders or services of worship which set forth an overall context in which hymns and other specific acts of worship can find their place. This practice is continued in the opening section of *The United Methodist Hymnal*, entitled "General Services." The "Basic Pattern of Worship," "An Order of Sunday Worship Using the Basic Pattern," and the "Service of Word and Table" constitute the framework within which the other acts of worship in the hymnal take place.

Services of the Baptismal Covenant are also included in this opening section. The two sacraments, Baptism and the Lord's Supper, belong together; and both belong with the Word in the unity of Word and Sacrament. Furthermore, this prominent placement of Baptism, Confirmation, reaffirmation of faith, and church membership emphasizes our evangelistic task to win persons for Christ and the church.

The next section is entitled "Hymns, Canticles, Acts of Worship." This makes up the bulk of the hymnal and is a testimony to the crucial importance of hymns as a part of worship. These are discussed more fully in *The Hymns of The United Methodist Hymnal.*

Next is the Psalter. The greater coverage of the Psalms, and the new format with optional sung responses, witness to the greater attention that is being given today to the Psalms as the biblical book of praise for God's people.

Next come "A Service of Christian Marriage," "A Service of Death and Resurrection," and "Orders of Daily Praise and Prayer." These are in the hymnal because they are services likely to be held from time to time in sanctuaries or chapels where hymnals are available, and they require congregational participation.

Next are particular acts of worship that call for congregational participation—affirmations of faith, prayers of confession, the Lord's Prayer, and sung Amens.

Finally, there are indexes—of authors and composers, of the Scriptures cited in the hymns and worship resources, of meters and tune names, of topics and categories, and of first lines and common titles.

This arrangement of contents gives a unified structure both to our hymnal and to our worship.

# CHAPTER 2

# THE STORY OF THE NEW SERVICES

## A. The Process of Development

The 1984 General Conference adopted into the Ritual of The United Methodist Church a new set of General Services that were published in 1985 as *The Book of Services* and have now been included in this hymnal. They are found here as "The Basic Pattern of Worship," "An Order of Sunday Worship Using the Basic Pattern," "Services of Word and Table" (except for Service IV), "Services of the Baptismal Covenant" (except for Service III), "A Service of Christian Marriage," and "A Service of Death and Resurrection." Though these services are substantively the same as those in *The Book of Services*, they appear in the hymnal in an improved format.

These new services provide for the first time a set of official services developed by The United Methodist Church. The Ritual of The Methodist Church was last revised in 1964, and the Ritual of The Evangelical United Brethren Church was last revised in 1959. When these two denominations united in 1968 to form The United Methodist Church, the time was not ripe for a single United Methodist ritual. For that reason, *The Book of Discipline* 1968 (Par. 1388) provided that "the Ritual of the Church is that contained in the *Book of Ritual* of The Evangelical United Brethren Church, 1959, and *The Book of Worship for Church and Home* [1965] of The Methodist Church."

The 1968 General Conference also set up a Commission on Worship, two of whose functions were: "3. When need arises, to prepare forms of worship and to revise existing orders of

11

worship for recommendation to the General Conference. 4. To supervise future editions of *The Book of Worship for Church and Home*, as may be authorized by the General Conference." Since 1972 these functions have been assigned to the Section on Worship of the General Board of Discipleship.

The process of research, development, and testing that took place from 1968 to 1984 was the most extensive in the history of our Ritual. At each General Conference during these years, a full progress report was received and authorization was given for the work to continue. From 1972 through 1979 trial versions of each of these services were published by Abingdon Press and given wide circulation and trial use in large numbers of United Methodist congregations. This resulted in a great many helpful comments and suggestions, which guided the revision of these services. A revised trial version of these services was published in 1980 as the booklet *We Gather Together*. These revised services were commended by the 1980 General Conference to local churches for trial use, and The General Board of Discipleship was instructed to revise them in the light of this trial use and submit them to the 1984 General Conference for adoption into the Ritual of the Church. Another large body of helpful criticism and suggestions was received during the next four years, and each of the services was further revised for presentation to the 1984 General Conference. The whole process has been described in detail in the preface to *The Book of Services* (1985) and in *Companion to The Book of Services* (1988).

As a result of action taken by the 1976 General Conference, a new set of United Methodist ordination and consecration services was developed, submitted to the 1980 General Conference, and adopted into the Ritual of the Church.

By action of the 1984 General Conference (*The Book of Discipline*, Par. 1214.3), "The Ritual of the Church is that contained in the Book of Ritual of The Evangelical United Brethren Church, 1959, 'The General Services of the Church' in The Book of Worship for Church and Home of The Methodist Church, The Ordinal 1981, and 'The General Services of the Church 1984' (English and Spanish versions)."

The Hymnal Revision Committee set up by the 1984 General Conference was faced with the fact that the entire Ritual of the Church was much too lengthy to be included in the new hymnal. Decisions had to be made as to which services were needed by *the whole congregation* and should therefore be in the hymnal. A denomination-wide survey was taken as to what services should be included. The following decisions were made by the Committee and adopted by the 1988 General Conference:

1. The 1984 General Services (English version) should be included. They all require extensive congregational participation and need to be in the hymnal, if the people are to have access to them.

2. The 1984 General Services (Spanish version) are available elsewhere and do not need to be in the hymnal.

3. None of the ordination and consecration services needs to be in the hymnal, since these services are not local church functions.

4. Of the orders and services of worship inherited from the former Methodist and Evangelical United Brethren churches, only the services of Holy Communion, Baptism, and Confirmation involved congregational participation and needed to be in the hymnal. The Methodist and EUB services of Holy Communion were similar enough that they could be effectively combined into what appears in the new hymnal as "A Service of Word and Table IV." The EUB and Methodist services for the baptism of youth and adults and for confirmation and reception of members were readily combined into what appears in the new hymnal as "The Baptismal Covenant III." The Methodist and EUB services for the baptism of children could not readily be combined, and so the part of each service spoken by the people is included in the new hymnal. The older services for marriage and the burial of the dead were not in the 1957 EUB and 1964 Methodist hymnals, and need not be in the new hymnal, because they do not require congregational participation. These services are available in other books.

5. A widespread need was felt for orders of daily praise and prayer, although no such services are part of our existing Ritual. Accordingly, the Section on Worship of the Board of Disciple-

ship, in cooperation with the Hymnal Revision Committee, prepared new "Orders of Daily Praise and Prayer" for the hymnal.

## B. GUIDING PRINCIPLES

Several basic principles guided the development of the new services:

1. The primary principle throughout is the authority of Scripture. Every effort was made to develop each of these services in accordance with the teachings of Scripture and to avoid anything that is contrary to Scripture. John Wesley's admonition to the American Methodists "to follow the Scriptures and the primitive church"[2] in their worship has been taken with the utmost seriousness. The biblical roots of these services are described in the following chapters of this book.

2. These services are deeply traditional. In keeping with Wesley's respect for "the primitive church," the shape and content of the services are based on the oldest available Christian models and reflect the experience of the church through the centuries.

3. These services are thoroughly Wesleyan. They reflect careful research into Wesley's beliefs and practices regarding worship and into the traditions that have developed in churches of the Wesleyan heritage since Wesley's time.

4. These services are ecumenical. Following Wesley's own broad appreciation of the contributions of every branch of Christ's holy Church, these services have been informed by the contributions of the Church universal. Worship books and authorities from many denominations have been consulted and have made important contributions at every stage of the development of these services.

---

2. *John Wesley's Sunday Service of the Methodists in North America,* with an introduction by James F. White [A Methodist Bicentennial Commemorative Reprint from *Quarterly Review*] (Nashville: The United Methodist Publishing House and the United Methodist Board of Higher Education and Ministry, 1984), p. iii.

5. Within this essential unity, there is room for much diversity. These services are designed to be flexible, so that with appropriate adaptations they can be used in a variety of situations. United Methodist local churches range from very large to very small in membership, from very formal to very informal in worship style, with a wide variety of racial, ethnic, and cultural heritages. Some of our worship is heavily dependent upon reading from a hymnal or bulletin, while other worship makes little or no use of reading. Special care has been given to test and evaluate the suitability of these services in the widest variety of situations.

Even so, there will be situations where adaptations are needed that are not explicitly provided for in the services themselves. In such cases, pastors and other leaders of worship should know that they have Christian liberty to meet the pastoral needs of their congregations. At the same time, worship at any particular time and place should also respect the integrity of Christian worship and the common worship of the wider church.

6. Inevitably these services contain compromises at points where United Methodists are not of one mind. One especially difficult area throughout the years in which these services have been developed has been that of the tension between familiar usages and inclusive language. It has been the basic intention throughout the development of these services to avoid language that discriminates against—or is insensitive to—women, persons of any age or developmental level, any racial or ethnic community, or persons with handicapping conditions. Two particular guiding principles in this connection have been (a) not to use masculine language to refer to people in general and (b) to seek a balanced diversity of scriptural imagery in addressing or referring to God. In practice, however, there have been frequent disagreements about particular usages. Many active participants in the development process would have preferred wording different from that which now appears. These services as they stand represent the best resolution possible for our denomination at this time, and they are offered to the church in the spirit of Christian liberty referred to above.

7. The services in the new hymnal will be supplemented, not only by resources already available but by further publications. Suggestions for future worship resources are welcomed by the Section on Worship.

May these services be used to the glory of God and the proclamation of the gospel of Jesus Christ.

# CHAPTER 3

# THE BASIC PATTERN OF WORSHIP

## A. WHAT IS A BASIC PATTERN?

"The Basic Pattern of Worship" is rooted in Scripture and in our heritage and experience as United Methodists. It is neither an order of worship nor something to be followed by the people during worship as a substitute for a bulletin. It serves, rather, to guide those who plan worship and to help persons in the congregation understand that behind the diversity of United Methodist worship there is a basic unity.

United Methodist worship is a balance of order and freedom. This balance is in large measure rooted in our understanding that worship should (1) have biblical structure and content, and (2) be a natural expression of the worshiping congregation.

On the one hand, we are proud of our heritage of freedom. We affirm the right of congregations to worship in different ways. We rejoice that churches of large and small membership, in different regions, in different types of community, of different racial and ethnic composition, and with distinctive local traditions can each worship in a style that "comes naturally" and enables the people to feel "at home."

But freedom is not anarchy or license. We have also affirmed the need for order, based on the teachings of Scripture and the message of the gospel. There is a basic pattern to our worship that has proved itself over the generations and centuries.

The early Methodists in America struggled to balance order and freedom in their worship.

In 1784 John Wesley sent them his *Sunday Service of the*

*Methodists in North America,* based on *The Book of Common Prayer* of the Church of England. While it was certainly biblical, American Methodists found that it did not "speak their language." They did not feel "at home" with it.

Wesley himself wrote, in the letter that accompanied his *Sunday Service:* "Our American brethren . . . are now at full liberty, simply to follow the Scriptures and the primitive church. And we judge it best that they should stand fast in that liberty, wherewith God has so strangely made them free."[3]

In 1792, under the leadership of Francis Asbury, the American Methodists adopted a more flexible basic pattern: "Let the morning service consist of singing, prayer, the reading of one chapter out of the Old Testament, and another out of the New, and preaching."[4] When Holy Communion was celebrated, Wesley's text, in a shortened form that began with the offering, completed the service. With a few changes such as the addition of the Lord's Prayer and the benediction, this was the official pattern for approximately the next century, during which Methodists experienced their greatest period of growth. Evangelicals and United Brethren during this period had a similarly flexible pattern of worship.

In the closing years of the nineteenth century, and during the early and middle twentieth century, the denominations that now make up The United Methodist Church moved from a basic pattern to an increasingly detailed order of worship. This was a significant change. In the basic pattern, the mention of "singing," for example, was a statement of what should be *included.* It could be interpreted according to the needs of the occasion to mean a single opening hymn, an opening "song service," or hymns scattered through the service. In an order of worship, on the other hand, it was specified *when* in the service a hymn should be sung. To be sure, there is a sequence implied in a basic pattern and some flexibility in most orders of worship, but there is clearly a difference of emphasis.

---

3. *John Wesley's Sunday Service of the Methodists in North America,* with an introduction by James F. White [A Methodist Bicentennial Commemorative Reprint from *Quarterly Review*] (Nashville: The United Methodist Publishing House and the United Methodist Board of Higher Education and Ministry, 1984), p. iii.
4. *The Doctrines and Discipline of the Methodist Episcopal Church* 1792, part I, section XXIII, pp. 40-41.

Now that we have had orders of worship for about a century, it seems clear that there is a place in United Methodism for *both* a basic pattern and for orders of worship. For this reason, *The United Methodist Hymnal* contains both "The Basic Pattern of Worship" and "An Order of Sunday Worship Using the Basic Pattern." Providing an order of worship as a specific model meets many needs, and our wide use of orders of worship in the twentieth century is testimony to this fact. On the other hand, the fact that no one order of worship can include and affirm the wide variety of United Methodist worship has led to calls for a more flexible basic pattern. Accordingly, the United Methodist services adopted by the 1984 General Conference and included in the new hymnal begin with "The Basic Pattern of Worship," followed by orders and texts that illustrate ways—but by no means the only ways—in which this pattern can be followed in actual services.

## B. BIBLICAL BASIS

This Basic Pattern is not new. It is thoroughly biblical. It is rooted in worship as Jesus and his earliest disciples knew it—services in the synagogue and family worship around the meal table. It has been "fleshed out" by the experience and traditions of Christian congregations as they have worshiped through the centuries.

Our preaching service, or "Service of the Word," is adapted from the synagogue service as Jesus knew it. The word *synagogue* means "gathering" or "assembly" and was applied first to gatherings or assemblies centered in readings from the Scriptures and teaching based on these readings, interspersed with praise and prayer. Later the term was applied also to the houses built to accommodate these assemblies.

It is significant how much of Jesus' preaching and teaching was done in synagogues, in the context of worship (Matt. 4:23; 9:35; 12:9 ff.; 13:54 ff.; Mark 1:21 ff., 39; 3:1 ff.; 6:2 ff.; Luke 4:15 ff., 31 ff., 44; 6:6 ff.; 13:10 ff.; John 7:59; 18:20). In Jesus' hometown of Nazareth, for instance, "he went to the synagogue, as his custom was, on the sabbath day," read Isaiah

61:1-2 from the Scriptures, and then preached to those assembled (Luke 4:16 ff.).

Our Holy Communion or "Service of the Table" is also biblical. As Jesus and his disciples traveled together, they also ate together. As devout Jews, they considered these meals sacred occasions to be observed with thanksgiving to God. The family meal table had long been the center of Jewish family worship. Jesus and his disciples, having left their families to travel together, had themselves become a family.

Jesus' supper with his disciples on the night before his death was both the last of these meals and the beginning of a transformed meal that Christians have eaten ever since. That night Jesus added something new to the sacred family meal they had known. As he gave them the bread he said, "This is my body. . . . Do this in remembrance of me." As he gave them the cup he said, "This is my blood . . . . Do this, as often as you drink it, in remembrance of me" (Matt. 26:26 ff.; Mark 14:22; Luke 22:19-20; I Cor. 11:23 ff.). The word we translate "remember" might better be translated "recall" in the sense of "call back": "Do this to call me back."

When Jesus was killed, his disciples were scattered; but two days later, on the first Easter, they found themselves face to face with the living, risen Christ. Ever since, Christian worship of God has been through encounter with the risen Christ. Christians have been an Easter people.

Luke 24:13 ff. describes the encounter of the disciples with the living Christ in a way that suggests a transformed synagogue service and a transformed holy meal. When the two disciples walking from Jerusalem to Emmaus had been joined by Jesus and had poured out their hearts to him, he quoted to them extensively from "Moses and all the prophets" (major sections of the Scriptures that Christians call the Old Testament) and *interpreted* these scriptures to them, a term that to Luke's readers would indicate what was done in the synagogue and its Christian equivalent. When they got to Emmaus and sat down to their evening meal, Jesus began to do what he had done before at such meals. "He took the bread and blessed, and broke it, and gave it to them. And their eyes were opened and they

recognized him. . . . He was known to them in the breaking of
the bread" (Luke 24:30, 35). Again, later that evening in Jerusalem, he appeared to a larger group of disciples, ate in their
presence, and "opened their minds to understand the Scriptures" (v. 45).

John's Gospel (chapters 20–21) tells not only that the risen
Christ ate breakfast with his disciples, but also that Thomas,
when he met the risen Christ, said, "My Lord and my God!"
Ever since, Christians have experienced encounters with the
risen Christ as encounters with God.

We read that Jesus then ascended into heaven, is at the right
hand of God, and "fills all in all" (Acts 1:9-11; Eph. 1:20-23). He
promised his disciples "I am with you always" (Matt. 28:20). Just
as God is everywhere and can be encountered and worshiped
anywhere, so also can the risen and ascended Christ.

Acts 1 and 2 records Jesus' promise at his ascension, "You
shall receive power when the Holy Spirit has come upon you,"
and its fulfillment on the day of Pentecost. From that day to this,
Christian worship has been an encounter with the living God
through the risen Christ in the power of the Holy Spirit. This is
one definition of Christian worship.

After the day of Pentecost (Acts 2), when the disciples went
out preaching and teaching with the power of the Holy Spirit,
they continued to take part in synagogue worship wherever
they went (Acts 9:2, 20; 13:5, 13 ff., 44 ff.; 14:1; 17:1 ff., 10 ff.,
17 ff.; 18:4, 19, 26; 19:8; 22:19; 24:12; 26:11) and to break bread as
a holy meal in their own gatherings (Acts 2:42, 46).

Their preaching and teaching about Jesus led to a break
between church and synagogue, and the Christians began to
hold their own adaptation of the synagogue service when they
gathered on the first day of the week for "the breaking of bread."
Interspersed with reading and preaching the Word of God,
these Christians would, we gather, "sing psalms and hymns
and spiritual songs with thankfulness . . . to God" (Col. 3:16).
This adapted synagogue service became the first part of the
combined service and came to be called the *synaxis*—a word that,
like *synagogue*, means "gathering." Such a combined service of
Word and Table is described in Acts 20:7 ff. and was apparently

an accepted pattern by the time Luke wrote. As noted biblical scholar Norman Perrin writes of Luke 24, "These narratives, especially the Emmaus road narrative, promise the reader that he or she can know Jesus as risen in the Eucharist" (Service of Word and Table).[5]

Since New Testament times, this basic pattern has had a long history of development. There have been times when this pattern has been obscured and corrupted, and times when it has been recovered and renewed. For those interested in this history, it is traced in *Companion to The Book of Services*, pages 31 ff. But through all this history the basic biblical pattern has constantly reasserted itself and is today the basis for the services in our hymnal.

## C. THE BASIC PATTERN EXPLAINED

The basic pattern consists of four parts: (1) Entrance, (2) Proclamation and Response, (3), Thanksgiving and Communion, and (4) Sending Forth. The "outer" parts (1 and 4) are the opening and closing, which are crucial parts of any gathering or assembly. The "inner" or central parts (2 and 3) are the Service of the Word and the Service of the Table, whose biblical roots in synagogue and at table we have just examined.

1. The *Entrance* (more formally referred to in some traditions as "The Entrance Rite") calls to mind Psalm 100: "Come into [God's] presence with singing! . . . Enter [God's] gates with thanksgiving, and [God's] courts with praise!"

When the people come together in the name of the Lord God and of the Lord Jesus Christ, it is natural that there be greetings—to one another in the Lord's name and to the Lord with prayer and praise. Greetings to one another may be totally spontaneous and informal as the people gather. They may also be formal and elaborate exchanges between leader, choir, and congregation. Greetings to the Lord take the form of prayer and praise, which also may be formal or informal.

---

5. Norman Perrin, *The Resurrection According to Matthew, Mark, and Luke* (Philadelphia: Fortress Press, 1977), pp. 76-77.

It is also natural that we "come into God's presence with singing" and instrumental music. Praise and prayer to God are particularly effective when sung; and, as Psalm 150 reminds us, instrumental music can also be praise to God.

The Entrance can take forms as diverse as a single opening prayer or hymn, an opening song service, or the more complex pattern found in "An Order of Sunday Worship." It can, however, easily become *too* complex. As the preface to the service of the Word, it should prepare the way for, and enhance, the proclamation of the Word.

2. In the *Proclamation and Response,* as in the synagogue service that Jesus knew, the Scriptures are opened to the people through the reading of lessons and preaching. There are other ways of opening the Scriptures to the people. Lay speaking or witnessing can testify to the meaning and power of God's Word. Singing can effectively proclaim Scripture texts or witness to Scripture teachings. Bible stories or characters can be dramatized. Visuals, ranging from stained-glass windows to banners and projections, can help open up the meaning of Scripture, as can actions, movement, and gestures.

From the earliest times, the reading and preaching of Scripture have been the heart of the Church's mission. This pattern of worship is designed to reassert the primacy of Scripture and the direct relation of the Scripture to preaching and response.

Proclamation calls forth response. Interspersed with acts of proclamation may be psalms, anthems, and hymns. Proclamation should invite the congregation to acts of commitment and faith with offerings of concerns, prayers, gifts, and service for the world and for one another. While there are varieties of ways in which worship may be ordered to accomplish this, it is natural that there be a rhythm of call-and-response. Examples of this rhythm are found in "An Order of Sunday Worship" and "A Service of Word and Table I."

Those who participated in the testing of this basic pattern in its trial period will remember that what is now a single section called "Proclamation and Response" was at first two sections: "Proclamation and Praise," followed by "Responses and

Offerings." Testing among United Methodists, ecumenical consultation, and further reflection revealed that such a division broke up what should be experienced as a unity and failed to acknowledge that there were responses after scripture readings as well as after the sermon.

3. *Thanksgiving and Communion* can take one of two basic forms.

When Holy Communion is celebrated, we reenact the actions of Jesus in the Upper Room: (1) As Jesus took the bread and the cup, so do we; (2) as Jesus gave thanks over the bread and the cup, so do we; (3) as Jesus broke the bread, so do we; and (4) as Jesus gave the bread and cup to his disciples, so we give them to one another. Since the first and third of these actions are very brief and preliminary to the second and fourth, we may simplify these steps in two: (1) taking the bread and cup and giving thanks over them and (2) breaking the bread and giving the bread and cup to one another. These two steps we may call simply thanksgiving and communion. They are the most basic components of the sacrament of Holy Communion.

In services when Holy Communion is *not* celebrated, it is important that we include thanksgiving for God's mighty acts in Jesus Christ that have made us the body of Christ and given us communion with the living God in the power of the Holy Spirit. Just *how* we do this is less important than *that* we do this.

4. Our worship concludes with the *Sending Forth.* After acts of sending, such as a closing hymn and dismissal with God's blessing (benediction), the people go forth into ministry in the world.

## D. Worship as Encounter with the Risen Christ

As congregations experience weekly worship that draws upon the resources in the new hymnal, three impressions are likely to emerge strongly and may well need to be dealt with in preaching.

1. The proclamation of Scripture is not only more prominent but is treated as an encounter with the living Christ, calling for our response.

2. Our congregational responses to the call of Christ have become more specific and personal. The Psalter and the Concerns and Prayers are examples. Our thanksgiving and our laments, our petitions and our intercessions, are more openly and honestly stated.

3. Holy Communion is primarily a joyous sharing with the living, risen, and ascended Christ, rather than primarily a somber remembering of Jesus' death.

It may be particularly helpful in interpreting these new emphases to congregations to preach on the resurrection, ascension, and Holy Spirit events mentioned above, which are so crucial in understanding the character of Christian worship. The Great Fifty Days from Easter through the day of Pentecost are a good time to do this. A good place to start might be to look at the basic pattern of worship as a whole in the light of the disciples' encounter with the risen Christ on the first Easter in Luke 24:13-35.

As on the first day of the week the two disciples were walking together on the road to Emmaus and were joined by the risen Christ, whom they did not recognize, so on the first day of the week we come together as a congregation on the journey of our lives and are joined by the risen (and ascended!) Christ, who comes to us in the power of the Holy Spirit but whom we do not always recognize.

As this risen Christ encouraged those disciples to pour out their hearts to him, so the risen and ascended Christ encourages *us* when we gather to pour out *our* hearts. As those disciples poured out disillusionment and sadness, so may we if that is our condition. As those disciples later that evening poured out faith and joy when they gathered in Jerusalem and again met the risen Christ, so may we through our opening acts of greeting and praise. In any case, just as those disciples needed to share what was in their hearts—to "open up"—before they were ready to hear Jesus interpret God's Word to them, so may we by opening our hearts become ready to hear the Word.

As Jesus "opened the Scriptures" to those first disciples and their hearts burned within them, so we hear the Scriptures opened to us today and out of the burning of our hearts praise God.

As those disciples came to a point where a response was called for, so do we. They did not say good-bye to Jesus but invited him to stay with them, and we can do the same.

As the disciples and the risen Christ came together around the table, so can we. As Jesus did the same four actions with the bread that the disciples had seen him do just three days previously, so in the name of the risen Christ we do these actions with the bread and cup. As "he was known to them in the breaking of the bread," so the risen and ascended Christ can be known to us in the Holy Communion.

As the risen Christ disappeared and sent the disciples forth into the world with faith and joy, so the risen and ascended Christ sends *us* forth into the world. And as those disciples found Christ when they arrived at Jerusalem, so we can find that he is with us wherever we go.

# CHAPTER 4

# AN ORDER OF SUNDAY WORSHIP USING THE BASIC PATTERN

## A. INTRODUCTION

"An Order of Sunday Worship" fleshes out the basic pattern of worship into an outline of an actual service. This outline incorporates the experience and traditions of Christians through the centuries with particular care to include what is distinctive in our United Methodist heritage. It rests on the same biblical foundations as the basic pattern and, in addition, reflects the historical developments traced on pages 31 ff. of *Companion to The Book of Services*. It represents classic, traditional Christian and United Methodist worship in a form that shows the great variety possible within its framework.

While we affirm the freedom and diversity of United Methodist worship, which is more than can be incorporated into any single order of worship, we also affirm our heritage of order and the need of many for the specific guidance and modeling that an order of worship provides.

Like the basic pattern, this order is a guide for those who plan worship rather than a bulletin to be followed by the congregation. A congregation may be guided through its worship services either by a printed bulletin or by announcement, and this order affirms both styles. Worship may follow what is printed in a bulletin or hymnal, or it may rely for its direction on the persons who lead it. Most United Methodists prefer a mixture of the two styles, but the proportions of the mixture vary greatly from one congregation and occasion to another. A

27

hymnal by its very nature deals mostly with acts of worship that are read from the printed page; but this order of worship, like the basic pattern, affirms both styles of worship in any appropriate combination.

This order includes the same four major divisions as the basic pattern: Entrance, Proclamation and Response, Thanksgiving and Communion, and Sending Forth. Since we have discussed these above, we shall turn now to the specific items in the order.

## B. The Entrance

### GATHERING

*The people come together in the Lord's name. While they are gathering, one or more of the following may take place:*
(1) Informal greetings, conversation, and fellowship
(2) Announcements and welcoming
(3) Rehearsal of congregational music and other acts of worship
(4) Informal prayer, singing, testimony
(5) Quiet meditation and private prayer
(6) Organ or other instrumental or vocal music

The service of worship begins when the people begin to gather for worship. The acts of worship that we call the "gathering" include both what happens as people are entering the church and what happens after they are seated. This is not simply an ideal. The plain fact is that before the opening hymn is sung or the people are formally called to worship, the tone and spirit of the service has been set by the way in which the congregation has gathered. The fact that the Jewish word *synagogue* and the early Christian word *synaxis* both mean *gathering* shows that the crucial importance of *gathering* for worship has been recognized since ancient times.

What the people do as they are gathering should express in some appropriate way the fact that they are coming together in the Lord's name. This time is both an "outward and visible" gathering of the people, and also an "inward and spiritual" gathering—a putting aside of inner preoccupations, a "getting it all together," a focusing of awareness that they are a people gathered in the presence of the Lord. Even when a worship service immediately follows another activity such as Sunday school in the same room, and some persons who have been at the earlier activity simply remain seated for the worship that follows, the gathering is a crucial part of the worship service.

Informal greetings, conversation, and fellowship should have some appropriate place in the gathering. This renewing of community is a part of our entrance into congregational worship and should not be discouraged.

Some churches have been placing their announcements and welcoming of visitors during the gathering. These are not to be confused with prayer concerns, which appropriately belong later in the service. Many believe that announcements are less of an interruption here than later, and that visitors should be publicly welcomed as early as possible in the service to help them feel at home.

When new hymns or service music are being introduced, some churches like during the gathering to rehearse the congregation in any unfamiliar music that they will be asked to sing later in the service. This practice may become more common as congregations begin to use the new hymnal with all of its new music.

Many persons feel the need for quiet meditation and private prayer as part of their entry into worship. This may take place while organ or other instrumental or vocal music is being offered. It is important that such music be recognized as part of the worship service—an offering by the musician(s) to God on behalf of the entire congregation—rather than as a mere prelude to the worship service.

The six acts suggested above for the gathering may be combined in a variety of ways: (1) may be encouraged before (5) and (6) begin, or before persons have entered the place of worship. Five and (6) may take place together following (2), (3), or (4). Five may also take place in a separate prayer room or chapel. None of the recommended patterns or combinations in itself is more valid than another, but one may be far more *appropriate* than another, depending on the particular congregation and circumstances.

## GREETING AND HYMN

*Facing the people, the leader greets them in the Lord's name. Scripture sentences or responsive acts between leader and people declare that the Lord is present and empowers our worship. The hymn may precede or follow the greeting.*

This should be an explicitly Christian greeting. It is no mere secular greeting, such as exchanging, "Good morning." Nor is it, strictly speaking, a "call to worship," since using that term here would imply that the gathering was not part of the worship. In some churches the choir also sings a greeting to the congregation (sometimes called the "introit"), but this should not be a substitute for the greeting by the leader. The leader need not be the pastor, but may be a lay liturgist. A simple greeting, used over a period of time and easily memorized by the people, can be both natural and effective to serve this purpose.

The term "the Lord" means both the Lord God and the Lord Jesus Christ. We are called together in the name of the God revealed in Jesus Christ; and our communion with God is through the living, risen Jesus Christ.

It is appropriate that the people, having been greeted in the Lord's name, return the greeting to God with a hymn of praise. On the other hand, where the architecture of the worship space or the nature of the occasion calls for an entrance of choir and worship leaders, this processional hymn or entrance song should come *before* the greeting, allowing the greeting to be spoken facing the people rather than from behind them.

The opening hymn is most appropriately corporate praise to God. It appropriately centers on the principal attributes or deeds of God that call forth gratitude and praise. It may be related to the day or season in the Christian year, but always bear in mind that every Lord's Day (even in Lent!) is a joyous "little Easter." This hymn should normally be familiar, upbeat, and affirming. If it is a processional hymn, the rhythm and length of the hymn should be appropriate.

It is appropriate to stand during the singing of this hymn. If the hymn precedes the greeting, it is appropriate to remain standing for the greeting. Printed or oral invitations to stand, here or elsewhere in the service, should show sensitivity to the fact that some persons cannot stand. Phrases such as "are invited to stand" or "may stand," or the simple gesture of upturned palms, are more inclusive than words that sound like a command to stand or an assumption that everyone will stand.

## OPENING PRAYERS AND PRAISE

*One or more of the following may be spoken or sung:*

Prayer of the day, such as a collect
Prayer of confession and act of pardon
Litany, such as the "Lord, Have Mercy"

Prayer during the Entrance, together with singing addressed to God, establishes that our worship is a communion with God as well as with one another. It includes recognition of who we are before God by centering upon the nature and gifts of God.

If there is a *prayer of the day,* it may be a printed prayer such as one of the classic collects, or it may be an extemporaneous prayer. It may be a prayer suited to any occasion, or any Lord's Day; or it may address God in the light of the theme of the day or season of the Christian year. A collection of such prayers—some for general use and some for particular days, seasons, or occasions—are interspersed among the hymns in the hymnal. Additional opening prayers for general use are found on pages 34-36 of *The Book of Services,* listed in the Bibliography. This prayer may be prayed in unison or led by one person. It may be preceded or followed by silence.

If there is a *prayer of confession and act of pardon,* this may include (1) a formal or informal call to confession by the leader, (2) a prayer of confession prayed in unison by the people, (3) silence, and (4) words of assurance or declaration of pardon by the leader with perhaps a response by the people. A prayer of confession and declaration for pardon belong together; neither should be used without the other. Examples are printed in the hymnal under "Confession, Assurance, and Pardon" (Nos. 890-93) and "A Service of Word and Table" I and IV (Nos. 8 and 26-27).

Some hymns can serve as prayers of confession. Examples are listed under "Confession" in the hymnal's "Index of Topics and Categories" (Nos. 939-40 and 952).

Here or at some other appropriate point in the service may be a *litany*, or responsive prayer between leader and people. Litanies are not necessarily, or even usually, prayers of confession. The "Lord, Have Mercy" litany, found on pages 35-36 of *The Book of Services*, is an ancient treasure that is most appropriate here. The recurring lead-in line and response ("Let us pray to the Lord. **Lord, have mercy.**") may be sung (No. 485). If this is done, the leader may either speak the other lines or sing them on a single tone—the same "G" on which the following "let" will be sung. Contrary to common impression, the "Lord, Have Mercy" (*Kyrie Eleison*) is not a prayer of confession but wonderfully combines proclamation, praise, and supplication.

"Lord, Have Mercy" (*Kyrie Eleison*) may also be sung as a response to an opening prayer of the day or to a prayer of confession and act of pardon. Three settings are provided in the hymnal. The Taize *Kyrie* (No. 484) is the simplest, with one line repeated over and over by the community. The Orthodox *Kyrie* (No. 483) from the Russian Orthodox Church is longer and more majestic; a choir could introduce this by singing it once, with the congregation repeating it. The Kriewald *Kyrie* (No. 482), which may be sung in English translation, takes a call-and-response form, with a choir or soloist introducing each segment and the congregation repeating it.

This order is flexible with regard to the placement of confession and pardon. United Methodists have two traditions in this regard. Prior to 1964, the confession and pardon was always after the proclamation of the Word when Holy Communion was celebrated, and this remained the pattern in the 1964 brief form of Holy Communion. On the other hand, the order of Sunday worship without communion, which had not mentioned confession and pardon before 1932, began at that time to make provision for them near the opening of worship, following the pattern of Anglican Morning Prayer. This pattern was extended to the complete form of Holy Communion in 1964. While the printed texts of the Word and Table services in the hymnal place confession and pardon after the proclamation of the Word, this "Order of Sunday Worship" indicates that they may be placed at either point in the service.

It may make an important practical difference where confession is placed. When there is an opening prayer of confession, persons confess the sin that they are already aware of when they come to church, or they simply acknowledge their status before God as sinners saved by grace. Confession after the proclamation of the Word includes the added awareness of personal and corporate sin to which persons are led by the proclamation of the Word.

There is no single correct posture for the congregation during prayer. The biblical tradition of standing to pray is always appropriate, especially when the people stand for praise immediately before or after the prayer. Kneeling for prayer is also appropriate, especially in confession. Praying seated and bowed is acceptable, especially if the alternatives are for persons to be kept standing or kneeling for an uncomfortable length of time.

Whether a prayer is prayed aloud by the whole congregation or by a single leader, the "Amen" should be spoken or sung by the whole congregation. Sung "Amens" are found in the hymnal as Nos. 897-904. The word "Amen" means, "So be it." It is the people's expression of agreement with the prayer—their statement that this is *their* prayer.

*If an act of praise is desired, one or more of the following may be spoken or sung:*

The "Glory to God in the Highest"
A psalm or other scripture song
The Gloria Patri
An anthem

This is a point in the service where choirs commonly sing, though they may also sing between lessons or at the offering. Choir music can appropriately be sung at various points in the service, depending upon what is being sung. A musical text praising God for pardoning mercy, for instance, might be most fitting after confession and pardon. A musical text that is a prayer for others might best be placed with the spoken intercessions. A general anthem of praise might be appropriate at any of several points in the service. Wherever an anthem is placed, it should not break the rhythm or interrupt the flow of the service but should be an integral part of the worship. Because it is best, when possible, to include the whole congregation in acts of praise, there is a growing movement toward musical forms in which the whole congregation has a familiar or easily learned part to sing.

Ancient and biblical acts of praise are the most traditional at this point in the service, and there is much to be said for their use. These are more effective if sung by the whole congregation. Some, such as the Gloria Patri (Nos. 70-71), can be sung by any congregation. While some settings of "Glory to God in the Highest" are too difficult for most congregations to sing and are better suited to choirs, others such as Nos. 72 and 82-83 are suitable for congregational use.

Other possibilities for an act of praise at this point include a hymn, hymn stanza, chorus, doxology, or a spoken litany of praise.

## C. PROCLAMATION AND RESPONSE

### PRAYER FOR ILLUMINATION

*The blessing of the Holy Spirit is invoked upon the reading, preaching, hearing, and doing of the Word. This may be included with the opening prayers, if there has not been an act of praise.*

This prayer serves as a bridge between the Entrance and the Proclamation of the Word. In many churches this prayer is either prayed in unison by the congregation or led by a layperson. Some hymns or stanzas may also be sung as prayers for illumination; see "Prayer for Illumination" under "Service

Music" in the hymnal's "Index of Topics and Categories" (No. 951). See also Nos. 477, 493, and 602.

One way of simplifying this Order of Sunday Worship, especially if there is no choir, is to use an opening prayer that also serves as a prayer for illumination and go directly from the opening prayer to the reading of Scripture. Many traditional collects can serve this double purpose.

SCRIPTURE

*Two or three Scripture readings should be used. If there are not Old Testament, Epistle, and Gospel readings at each service, care should be taken that over a period of time the people hear representative readings from each.*

More Scripture is being read in worship today than was the case a few years ago. This is because the primacy of Scripture is being reasserted among United Methodists, and because we recognize that if the Bible is to exert its proper authority in the Church the people must know the stories and teachings that it contains. Since we live in a culture that is for the most part biblically illiterate, the only Scripture that many people will hear is what they hear in church. We saw above that the early American Methodists set out to evangelize the nation with a pattern of worship that included two full chapters of Scripture, balanced between the Old and New Testaments; and, while the letter of that pattern may have been rigid, we are seeking to recover its spirit.

But if a generous amount of Scripture is to be "opened" to the people, it must be done *well*. It must *not* be boring. Those who read Scripture in worship should practice these readings just as surely as choirs should rehearse anthems. Furthermore, Scripture can sometimes be presented in ways other than solo reading. The congregation may follow the reading silently in their own Bibles or in pew Bibles, or they may read a lesson in unison or in some responsive or antiphonal pattern. Several readers may dramatize a Bible story. Some Bible stories—the book of Esther, for instance—lend themselves better to retelling, perhaps in the first person, than to straight reading; and such retelling can often become effective preaching.

The historic practice of following a lectionary, or regular cycle of Scripture readings, has much to commend it. The three-year Common Lectionary includes for each Sunday a first reading (usually from the Old Testament), a second reading (usually from some part of the New Testament other than the Gospels), and a reading from one of the four Gospels. It is important to remember, however, that the lectionary is a means to an end, rather than an end in itself. A Bible story may take long enough to read or retell that it is not feasible to read two other Scripture passages that day. There may be reason to read and preach from a passage of Scripture not in the lectionary or appointed for some other time in the three-year cycle. Some preachers develop their own method of covering the story and teachings of the Bible. What is crucial is that over a period of time the congregation learn to know and love the story and teachings of the whole Bible.

When Scripture is read, the visual impact, as well as the sound, is important. Reading from a large pulpit Bible that all the people can see underscores the importance of Scripture. In some congregations, the Bible is brought in as part of the opening procession, placed on the pulpit, and opened at the beginning of the proclamation of the Word. When this Bible remains open in front of the preacher during the sermon, it emphasizes visually that the sermon comes from the Scriptures. On the other hand, to read the Scriptures from a (smaller) lectern rather than from the (larger) pulpit, and then walk away from the Bible to the pulpit to preach, symbolically diminishes the importance of Scripture. Lecterns should not be used for the reading of Scripture.

In many congregations, one or more of the Scripture lessons are read by a layperson. This follows ancient custom and is one of the ways laypersons can effectively share in the leadership of worship. Some laypersons are already highly effective readers, and others can become so through training. The booklet *Reading Scripture Aloud*, listed in the Bibliography, is a helpful resource. Many certified lay speakers serve as readers. By their careful preparation of the reading and by their sense of the importance of their ministry, readers of Scripture can make the reading of

Scripture among the high points of the service. Their ministry should be recognized and honored. It is both fair to all segments of the congregation and also more interesting and effective if the readers chosen over a period of time represent, in fair proportions, women and men, youth and young adults as well as middle and older adults, and whatever ethnic and cultural variety is in the congregation. The lay reader often sits in the congregation until time for the reading and then comes forward. This is a way of involving the congregation more closely in the reading and not separating the reader from family or from the rest of the people.

Special thought should be given to the words used to introduce and close the reading of Scripture. Introductory comments, explaining the setting of the readings, are often appropriate, but they should be very brief and to the point. Readings may be immediately preceded by such words as: "Hear the Word of God in a reading from _____." In closing, the reader may say, "This is the Word of the Lord," or simply, "The Word of the Lord," to which the people may respond, "Thanks be to God." Or the reader may say simply, "Amen," to which the people may respond, "Amen."

*The Scripture readings may be interspersed with:*

—A psalm or psalm portions, sung or spoken, after the first reading
—A hymn or song related to the Scriptures of the day, or a sung "alleluia," before the final reading

The use of an appropriate psalm or psalm portion as an act of praise is derived from ancient Jewish and Christian practice. When a psalm is used as an act of praise, it is appropriate for the people to stand. In this use, the psalms are not properly Old Testament lessons and should not be considered substitutes for the reading from the Old Testament. The Common Lectionary suggests a psalm for each Sunday or special day of the three-year cycle.

There is a variety of ways in which psalms may be spoken or sung as praise, and we are in an exciting time during which the psalms are being rediscovered as prayer and praise. The psalms are even more effective when sung than when spoken, and this hymnal opens up many new possibilities for singing the psalms. For further discussion of the Psalter, see chapter 7.

Traditionally an alleluia (Nos. 78, 186, and 486) has been sung before the reading of the Gospel, except during the preparatory seasons of Advent and Lent. This remains an effective practice today, and the return to singing "alleluia" on Christmas and Easter adds drama to those peak days of the Christian year. Notice how many Easter hymns include "alleluia." A hymn related to the Scriptures of the day may be sung in place of the "alleluia."

In either case, it is traditional for the people to be invited to stand for the singing and remain standing for the reading of the Gospel. In the Gospel, we are addressed by the words of Christ and in a special way experience this as an encounter with the risen, living Christ. To stand and greet Christ with an alleluia or hymn and remain standing while Christ speaks to us is an act of respect that has seemed natural to many Christians. It is not meant to imply that other portions of the Bible are less God's Word, nor should it be forced on congregations where it is not perceived as appropriate.

The rhythm of proclamation and response in this part of the service is a prime example of the call-and-response pattern that is so fundamental to our worship in general. God's Word comes to us through the reading of Scripture, and we respond with praise. Two specific patterns that we will encounter in "A Service of Word and Table I" illustrate this pattern:

| LONGER PATTERN | | SHORTER PATTERN | |
|---|---|---|---|
| *call* | *response* | *call* | *response* |
| Scripture | | Scripture | |
| | Psalm | | Hymn or Song |
| Scripture | | Scripture | |
| | Hymn or Song | | |
| Gospel | | | |

SERMON

*One or more of the Scripture readings are interpreted.*

On the road to Emmaus, Jesus "interpreted to them in all the scriptures the things concerning himself" (Luke 24:27). The verb we translate "interpreted" was used in New Testament times to refer to the preaching and teaching done in the synagogue services, and this verb still describes the task of the preacher regarding the Scriptures.

On the other hand, Jesus had sensitively listened as the disciples poured out the heaviness of their hearts (Luke 24:17-24); and thus he interpreted the Scriptures in ways that spoke specifically to their needs. So the effective preacher today is also a sensitive pastor who knows the condition and needs of the people.

The reading and preaching of the Bible are so closely related that nothing ought to come between them. To emphasize this unity, the ancient and ecumenical practice of placing the sermon immediately following the last Scripture reading is strongly recommended. Some ministers pray immediately before preaching; but, if one takes seriously the unity of Scripture reading and preaching, it would seem more fitting to invoke God's help in the prayer for illumination at the beginning of the whole Proclamation and Response section of the service.

When two or three Scripture passages have been read, it is not necessary to preach on both or all of them, although if they are closely related this is sometimes possible. It is enough to preach on one of them, and trust concerning the other passage(s) that God's Word will speak to the people through the reading itself. In some traditions, it is customary always to preach from the Gospel; but in others, such as ours, it is also appropriate to preach from one of the earlier readings or from the psalm.

Those who preach from the Common Lectionary will find that the three readings are usually linked, thematically or in some other fashion, from the Sunday before Advent (Christ the King) through the Sunday after Epiphany (Baptism of the Lord) and from the Sunday before Lent (Transfiguration Sunday) through

Easter Day. It may be quite possible to relate them all to the sermon.

During the rest of the year, except for occasional festivals or special days, this is not the case; and it is left for the preacher to choose which Scripture to preach from. During the half-year after Pentecost, each of the three readings goes from Sunday to Sunday in its own semicontinuous cycle, so that it is left to the preacher to choose whether to preach from the Old Testament cycle, the Epistle cycle, or the Gospel cycle. Thus, during that half of the year it is possible to find in the lectionary a nine-year preaching cycle.

Preaching is fully as important on Sundays when Holy Communion is celebrated as on other occasions. The omission of preaching on communion Sundays violates the unity of Word and Sacrament. A short sermon can be fully as important and effective as a long one and should not be called a "sermonette" or "meditation."

This does *not* mean that it is necessary to preach on the subject of Holy Communion every time it is celebrated; any facet of the gospel can be preached in such a way that it leads naturally to the celebration of Holy Communion. In fact, where misunderstanding of the Sacrament is causing persons to stay away on communion Sundays, it may be well to preach about Holy Communion when it is *not* being celebrated, so that those who especially need to hear the message will be more likely to be present.

The sermon is often strengthened by being conceived in flexible and imaginative terms. Dialogue, dramatization, visual accompaniment, use of objects, and active congregational participation are among the many possibilities for preaching. Lay speaking or lay witnessing, drama (live or on film or video tape), or a musical presentation that proclaims the Word can on occasion supplement, or take the place of, the sermon.

Some flexibility and imagination are particularly important as increasingly preachers welcome and recognize children in the worshiping congregation. Setting aside a time earlier in the service when the preacher speaks specifically with children (children's sermon, story, or dialogue) is a step toward full recognition of children in worship. A fuller recognition and involvement of children in worship comes when the sermon itself is preached in such a way that children as well as adults are interested and benefit. Perhaps the pastor who observes, "the adults get more out of my children's sermon than they do out of the main sermon," could begin bringing to the sermon some of the imagination and creativity that has made the moments with children so effective. Further help in fully incorporating children into worship services is found in the *God's Children in Worship Kit* and in the video cassette *Worship: Images Involving Children*, listed in the Bibliography.

## RESPONSE TO THE WORD

*Responses may include one or more of the following:*
Invitation to Christian discipleship, followed by a hymn of invitation or of response, or a baptism or confirmation hymn
Appropriate portions of the Baptismal Covenant:

Holy Baptism
Confirmation
Reaffirmation of Faith
Reception into The United Methodist Church
Reception into the Local Congregation
A creed, except when already used in the Baptismal Covenant

Preaching calls for a response. It is worship and evangelism in partnership. The ultimate response to God's Word is found in our daily faith and life, but an immediate response is also important. If we are to go out into our daily world as Christians, we need the strength and focus that comes from affirming our *commitment* to what has been proclaimed—our *ownership* of what we have heard. This vital part of the service is neglected in many congregations, and one of the chief concerns of this "Order of Sunday Worship" is to strengthen it. The book *Worship and Evangelism*, listed in the Bibliography, discusses in more detail how to do evangelism when using this Order.

Not only should the *content* of proclamation call for a

response, but the basic *call-and-response rhythm* of the service reinforces this call on several levels (or "frequencies"). (1) The whole "Proclamation and Response" part of the service falls in two major sections, with the crucial dividing point at the end of the sermon. Everything through the sermon is a great cumulative *call* for the responses that follow. (2) The back-to-back Gospel/Sermon sequence is itself a climactic call that should lead to an equally climactic time of response. (3) In some preaching traditions it is customary for the preaching itself to have a call-and-response rhythm, with spontaneous congregational responses punctuating the sermon. If we consider the "body language" of the congregation during preaching and the "feedback" this gives the observant preacher, it may be the case that *all* preaching involves constant call and response. Such frequent, brief responses—like the acts of praise in response to the earlier Scripture readings—rehearse the congregation for the time of response that follows the sermon.

The Response to the Word is an occasion for specific decision and witness. As indicated above, it includes a variety of possibilities.

The *invitation to Christian discipleship* is a bridge between the time of proclamation (call) and the time of response. The spoken invitation itself, given by the preacher, continues the Scripture/Sermon proclamation (call). The hymn that follows may be one of invitation (call), response, or a combination of both. This leads immediately to such responses as baptism, confirmation, profession or reaffirmation of faith, and reception into membership from another denomination or from another United Methodist congregation. More will be said about these acts in chapter 6. This invitation for commitment to Christ and his Church may also lead into installation and recognition services for church workers and officers, consecration and dedication services of all kinds, or other special congregational acts. Examples of such services are found in the book *Blessings and Consecrations* (Supplemental Worship Resources 14), published by Abingdon in 1984. This invitation may also lead to commitment to specific courses of action, into a time of silent reflection or spoken expressions from the congregation, or directly into the Concerns and Prayers of the church.

This is a most fitting time for a *creed or affirmation of faith*. On Sundays when a service of the Baptismal Covenant is used, it is appropriate that all those present be invited to reaffirm their faith at the time the Apostles' Creed is used. On other Sundays, the use of the Apostles' Creed (Nos. 881-82), the Nicene Creed (No. 880), a modern affirmation (Nos. 883-86), or a scripture affirmation (Nos. 887-89) at the same point in the service where a baptism would take place serves to remind us of our baptism and of the faith in which we were baptized. Some hymns lend themselves to being sung as affirmations of faith; see "Affirmation of Faith" in the hymnal's "Index of Topics and Categories" (No. 951, under "Service Music").

In this way *the whole congregation* can respond to the invitation to Christian discipleship with an act of faith and commitment. In most churches there are likely to be many Sundays when no one makes an individual response to the Word, and the fear that there will be a feeling of "letdown" on such days makes some pastors hesitant to call for a response to the Word. But such hesitation is needless. Whether or not there are additions to church membership on a given day, there can always be a powerful response to the invitation as God's people affirm their faith.

## CONCERNS AND PRAYERS

*Joys and concerns to be included in the prayers may be expressed. Prayer may take one or more of these forms:*

Brief intercessions, petitions, and thanksgivings by the leader or members of the congregation
Each of these prayers may be followed by a common response, such as, "Lord, hear our prayer," spoken or sung by all
Litany of intercession and petition
Pastoral prayer
*During this time persons may be invited to kneel at the communion rail.*

When Holy Communion is *not* celebrated, many congregations go immediately from the above Response to the Word to the Dismissal with Blessing and Going Forth. They may find it strange to have a climactic time of prayer and offering at this point in the service. It may not be possible for a congregation using the new hymnal to go to this "Order of Sunday Worship" without some adaptations at this point, at least during a time of transition.

In such a situation, here is a possible compromise or transitional step. The Opening Prayers may be expanded to include this time of concerns and prayers, general thanksgiving, and the Lord's Prayer. The offering may be placed after the Opening Prayers and before the Proclamation and Response. This arrangement at least keeps the reading and preaching of the Scriptures together and avoids the major problems that arise when they are separated.

There are, however, compelling reasons to recommend the historic and ecumenical practice of placing these acts of prayer and offering as response to the proclamation rather than with the prayers and praise in the Entrance.

1. Intercessions, petitions, and thanksgivings can better be made after the congregation has been prepared by the proclamation of the Word. The people will have been informed, sensitized, and motivated to be more aware of the joys and needs of the world and of the Church. At the opening of the service, on the other hand, the people are much less ready to bring these joys and needs before God in prayer.

2. Prayer is the most important and powerful immediate response that we can make to God's Word. An extensive and powerful proclamation of the Word calls for an extensive and powerful response by the whole congregation, centering in prayer. To limit prayer largely to the first part of the service fails to do justice to the importance of prayer in worship, as well as limiting the ability of persons and congregations to respond to the Word.

3. When acts of commitment such as those mentioned under Responses to the Word have just taken place, it is important that the congregation pray for and with the persons involved. This placement of the Concerns and Prayers gives the opportunity to do just that.

4. These prayers are a bridge between the hearing of the Word and the long-term response to the Word—which is found in changed lives, Christian growth, and Christian action in the world. They build on the foundation of the Word as it has been proclaimed and heard and of the basic Christian confessions of faith that have just been made in the Response to the Word; and they make these more concrete and specific in prayer. Christian life and work during the week that follows both begins with these specific prayers and is informed by them. Often God will call us to be part of the answers to our prayers.

Looking now at the Concerns and Prayers time itself, some United Methodists know this as the Pastoral Prayer, but the phrase "Concerns and Prayers" better indicates that the whole church family, not simply the pastor, is at prayer.

Before the time of prayer itself, persons in the congregation may be invited to express joys and concerns that they would like included in the prayers. If the congregation is too large for persons to be heard when they speak out, prayer requests may be written on cards and either deposited in an appropriately marked box or brought forward by ushers. Alternatively, prayer requests may be written on sheets posted in some appropriate location and marked "Prayer Requests." Persons may also express their prayer requests personally to the pastor or to the church office during the week or before the service.

The time of prayer itself should include any joys and concerns that have been expressed and may take any of the forms mentioned. The size and character of the congregation and of the space in which they worship will help indicate which of these forms is most practicable and effective.

An invitation to prayer quietly sung by choir or congregation (see No. 951 under "Invitation to Prayer") can be an effective preparation for prayer.

An "Amen" (Nos. 897-904) or a response following prayer (see No. 952 under "Prayer Responses") can be the people's "Amen" to the prayers. For this reason, it is better that this be sung by the whole congregation rather than by choir alone.

It is crucial that these be the prayers of the congregation, whether expressed directly by the people or indirectly through the one leading the prayer, and that they be seen and experienced as such by the people. This is a time for prayers that are as specific as possible—intercessions for persons or causes, petitions for particular needs, and thanksgivings for recent blessings. Where the people can participate with their spontaneous concerns and prayers, it adds freshness and life to the worship.

The custom of inviting persons to kneel at the communion rail during the congregation's intercessions, petitions, and thanksgivings will be unfamiliar to some congregations but is cherished tradition in others. This invitation is often called "the altar call," although others apply that term to the invitation to Christian discipleship.

There are also situations where, in addition to or instead of a prayer or prayers composed for the particular occasion, a general litany of intercession and petition is appropriate. Two such litanies are found on pages 39-41 of *The Book of Services*, listed in the Bibliography.

## CONFESSION, PARDON, AND PEACE

*A prayer of confession and act of pardon are used here, if not used during the Entrance.*

*The people may offer one another signs of reconciliation and love, particularly when Holy Communion is celebrated.*

The sequence of Confession and Pardon has already been discussed under Opening Prayers and Praise. Examples are found in Services of Word and Table I (No. 8), II (No. 12), and IV (Nos. 26-27) and in the collection of acts of worship entitled "Prayers of Confession, Assurance, and Pardon" (Nos. 890-93).There are several considerations in favor of placing this sequence at this point in the service:

1. Persons and congregations are likely to be more aware of their personal and corporate sin after hearing the Word proclaimed than they were at the beginning of the service.

2. The larger sequence of invitation, confession, pardon, peace, and offering is so scriptural and powerful, as we shall see below, that significant meaning is lost when it is broken up.

3. This larger sequence is particularly appropriate when it

serves as a bridge between the Service of the Word (Proclamation and Response) and the Service of the Table (Holy Communion). When Holy Communion is to follow, the invitation effectively serves both as invitation to communion and as call to confession, and the sequence as a whole serves as preparation for communion.

Let us look at this sequence more closely.

1. *The invitation* (or Call to Confession) expresses Christ's loving invitation to repent of our sin, live in peace with one another, and (if Holy Communion follows) join him at his table.

2. *The confession* acknowledges our sinfulness, not only as individuals but as a church and as participants in the wider society, and prays that as a forgiven people we may grow in the Spirit of Christ.

3. The *words of assurance* or *declaration of pardon* declares God's pardoning and empowering love.

4. *The peace.* Having made or renewed peace with God through confession and pardon, the people are now ready to make or renew peace with one another.

5. When the peace is to be followed immediately by *the offering,* we recall Jesus' words in Matthew 5:23-24: "If you are offering your gift at the altar, and there remember that your brother [or sister] has something against you, leave your gift there before the altar and go; first be reconciled to your brother [or sister], and then come and offer your gift."

Because the peace is new to many people, and can be an uncomfortable experience for some, it needs special interpretation. It is *not* simply greetings all around and general pleasantries. It is *not* the same thing as "the ritual of friendship." It is quite different from the greetings we exchange during the Gathering and the Going Forth. It is an act of reconciliation and blessing, based on the New Testament Christian practice of exchanging the peace ("a holy kiss," "the kiss of love"), as mentioned in Romans 16:16; I Corinthians 16:20; II Corinthians 13:12; I Thessalonians 5:26; I Peter 5:14. Since peace is the gift of God's grace through Jesus Christ, it is not simply *our* peace but the peace of *Christ* that we are offering one another.

The gestures and words used may vary widely, depending on

the character of the congregation and the nature of the occasion. For some, it will be a gesture primarily of love, for others primarily of reconciliation. Depending on the seating arrangement and the degree of intimacy perceived as authentic for the people, this act may consist in a simple handshake, a clasping of both hands, an embrace, or a kiss. The words used may be elaborate ("The peace of the Lord be with you." "And also with you.") or simply ("Peace." "Amen."). They may also be spontaneous, as individuals are moved. The invitation to exchange the peace may include an invitation to stand, and most persons are likely to exchange the peace while standing; but there should be sensitivity to those who are unable to stand or who prefer to remain seated. The intensity and significance of the peace may vary from time to time, and genuine differences of temperament and conviction should be respected.

OFFERING

*An offering may include:*

Monetary gifts
Other appropriate gifts,
    such as memorial gifts or other items to be dedicated
The bread and wine, if Holy Communion is to follow

*As the gifts are received and presented, there may be:*

A hymn
An anthem
A doxology or other musical response

The offering is more than money. It is the symbolic offering to God of ourselves and all that we have. It is the corporate self-giving of God's people, in the spirit of Romans 12:1: "Offer yourselves as a living sacrifice to God, dedicated to [God's] service and pleasing to [God]" (GNB, alt.). Offerings in addition to money might include, for instance, a commitment to a particular task, a talent sheet, or a letter to an appropriate government official about some issue. This is the mystery of giving back to God the gifts of God's creation, including signs of our labor, so that we know that all we have and are is a trust from God.

This symbolism is the basis for recommending that the offering be a response to the Word rather than preliminary to the Word. Many persons have strong feelings against this placement of the offering, however; and, if necessary, it may be placed between the Entrance and the Proclamation and Response.

If Holy Communion is to follow, the bread and wine are brought to the Lord's table—or uncovered, if already in place—by representatives of the people. It is important to symbolize that these fruits of the earth represent offerings of the people. They are the climax of the offering and should be presented after the money or other gifts.

While the offering is being received, there may be instrumental or choral music or congregational singing. When the offering is brought forward and laid on the Lord's table, it is fitting that the congregation stand and that a doxology (stanza of praise to the Trinity) or other appropriate stanza be sung. See "Doxology" under "Service Music" in the index No. 951.

## D. THANKSGIVING

### WITH HOLY COMMUNION

*The pastor prepares the bread and cup.*
*The pastor and people join in the Great Thanksgiving.*
*All pray the Lord's Prayer.*
*The pastor breaks the bread and lifts the cup.*
*The bread and cup are given to the people.*
*The congregation may sing hymns.*
*The table is set in order.*
*There may be a brief prayer.*

The basic pattern of Holy Communion has already been outlined in chapter 3. A detailed explanation of the steps in Holy Communion will be given in chapter 5.

## WITHOUT HOLY COMMUNION

*A prayer of thanksgiving is offered.*
*All pray the Lord's Prayer.*

On occasions when Holy Communion is *not* celebrated, the service may still incorporate the dimension of thanksgiving for all God's mighty acts in Jesus Christ that is supremely expressed in Holy Communion. As stated above, just *how* we do this is less important than *that* we do this.

In "An Order of Sunday Worship," a prayer of thanksgiving immediately follows the offering. While it has been common to follow the presentation of the offering with a prayer, this prayer has often had too narrow a focus. It is not a blessing of the money, but a blessing of God for the good news that is the gospel. The focus should not be on the money but on the reality and mighty acts of God in Jesus Christ.

This follows from the fact that the offering is more than money. We are able to offer ourselves and all that we have to God because God has first created us, given us all that we have, made the supreme offering to us in Jesus Christ, made us the body of Christ, and empowered us with the Holy Spirit. After we have thanked God for all this, our thanksgiving is completed by grateful reconsecration to life and service as Christian disciples.

Such a prayer reflects what is prayed in Holy Communion and anticipates the next celebration of Holy Communion.

In congregations that place the offering earlier in the service, this prayer might either (1) follow the offering, earlier in the service, or (2) be the concluding act in the response to the Word.

There are no examples of such a prayer in the hymnal, since it is prayed by the pastor and does not need to be printed in front of the people. Examples are to be included in the service book for pastors and other leaders of worship, now under development. Many pastors will prefer to compose such prayers themselves. Meanwhile, here are some examples that illustrate the range of possible styles:

1. The Great Thanksgiving as found on Nos. 9-10 or 13-14 can be used, including the introductory dialogue and congrega-

tional responses, but *omitting* those parts that pertain only to Holy Communion—i.e., the paragraphs beginning "on the night . . . ," "when the supper was over . . . ," and "pour out your Holy Spirit."

2. A freer adaptation of the Great Thanksgiving, such as this:

All things come from you, O God, and with praise and
    thanksgiving we return to you what is yours.
You created all that is, and lovingly formed us in your image.
When our love failed, your love remained steadfast.
You gave your only Son Jesus Christ to be our Savior,
    that we might have abundant and eternal life.
All that we are, and all that we have, is a trust from you.
And so, in gratitude for all that you have done,
we offer you ourselves and all that we have,
    in union with Christ's offering for us.
By your Holy Spirit make us one with Christ, one with one
    another, and one in ministry to all the world;
through Jesus Christ our Lord. **Amen.**

3. A classic prayer, such as this:

Almighty God, Father of all mercies,
we thine unworthy servants do give thee most humble and
hearty thanks for all thy goodness and loving-kindness to us,
and to all the world.
We bless thee for our creation, preservation,
    and all the blessings of this life,
but above all for thine inestimable love
    in the redemption of the world by our Lord Jesus Christ,
    for the means of grace, and for the hope of glory.
And we beseech thee, give us that due sense of all thy mercies,
    that our hearts may be unfeignedly thankful,
    and that we may show forth thy praise,
    not only with our lips, but in our lives,
    by giving up ourselves to thy service
    and by walking before thee in holiness and righteousness
    all our days;

through Jesus Christ our Lord,
  to whom, with thee and the Holy Spirit,
  be all honor and glory, world without end.
**Amen.**[6]

The unison praying of the Lord's Prayer, the most sublime
Christian prayer, expresses that communion with God which is
the climax of our worship. It may be sung by the congregation
(Nos. 270-71), but this supreme Christian prayer should not be
taken away from the people by a choir or soloist. A time of
silence may follow the Lord's Prayer, where breaking the bread
and giving the bread and cup would be if Holy Communion
were being celebrated. This can be a silent sharing (*koinonia*,
communion) with God, which suggests and echoes the sharing
with God in Holy Communion.

## E. Sending Forth

### HYMN OR SONG AND DISMISSAL WITH BLESSING

*Facing the people, the leader declares God's blessing.*
*The hymn may precede or follow the blessing.*

Whether or not Holy Communion has been celebrated, the
service concludes with a series of acts that are referred to as the
Sending Forth. It is appropriate that the congregation stand for
these, since they are about to scatter into active ministry in the
world.
A final hymn or song of sending forth may be one of
thanksgiving and praise or of consecration to service in the
world. It need not be an entire hymn, but may simply be one or
more stanzas. In some circumstances, spontaneous song or
spoken praise is appropriate. Many congregations sing a
favorite hymn, "theme song," stanza, or doxology (stanza of

---

6. From *The Book of Common Prayer*, 1928, slightly altered.

praise to the Trinity) at this point in every service. See the "Doxology"under "Service Music" in the index No. 951.

This hymn should not, however, be confused with the invitation hymn immediately following the sermon. Each has its appropriate place, but their purposes are quite different. Whereas an invitation hymn such as "Just as I Am" (357) *invites persons into the church,* a hymn of sending forth such as "Go, Make of All Disciples" (571) *sends persons into the world.*

The dismissal with blessing, often called the benediction, is given by the pastor to the people, face to face. It is addressed to the people, not to God; and the pastor and people should be looking at each other as it is being given. For this reason, it should be given by the pastor from the front, not the back, of the church. Thus, if the final hymn is a recessional in which the pastor joins, it should follow the dismissal with blessing. Otherwise, the dismissal with blessing follows the final hymn or song.

It is appropriate for the congregation to stand for the final hymn and the dismissal with blessing. This "body language" expresses the readiness and willingness of the people to go forth into the world as Christ's representatives.

GOING FORTH

*One or more of the following may be included:*

Organ or other instrumental voluntary
Silence before the congregation disperses
Informal greetings, conversation, and fellowship

The congregation then goes forth to continue its service to God in the life of the world. Like the gathering, this going forth is an act of corporate worship as long as people are still with other people in the place of worship. The sharing of informal greetings, conversation, and fellowship is already customary in most United Methodist congregations and reflects the spirit of the "peace."

The appropriate role of an organ or other instrumental voluntary depends on circumstances. Some churches omit it and let the final hymn be the musical climax. If a voluntary is offered, it should be as an offering to God on behalf of the entire congregation, recognized as part of the worship service and not regarded as a mere postlude following the worship. It may be music designed to accompany the going forth of the people—an instrumental recessional or "walking music" for the scattering of the people into the world. Or, it may be designed for listening before the people begin to move and converse. In the latter case, a problem may arise if people are asked to sit down again after having stood up and been dismissed—a sequence many find awkward and unnatural. Many congregations encourage the people to feel free during the playing of the voluntary either to (1) go forth, (2) remain standing quietly in place listening, or (3) sit down to listen. In any event, this music should be selected and played in such a way as to send the people "on their way rejoicing."

As the congregation goes forth, their ministry scattered in the world can be rooted in that communion with the living God and the community of faith which is the essence of worship.

# CHAPTER 5

# SERVICES OF WORD AND TABLE

## A. Introduction

Four Services of Word and Table are provided in the hymnal. They all follow the Basic Pattern and Order of Sunday Worship, but they do so in four distinct styles so as to meet the diverse needs of United Methodists in celebrating Holy Communion.

Most of the time, United Methodist congregations are guided through their worship services by a bulletin or by announcement; but when Holy Communion is celebrated, United Methodists have a long tradition of turning to the "Ritual" found in their hymnals. At services with Holy Communion, some United Methodists have the tradition of following the Ritual for the entire service, while other United Methodists worship in their accustomed fashion through the Service of the Word ("preaching service") and then turn to the "Brief Form" in the Ritual for Holy Communion itself.

These practices are rooted in our denominational history. John Wesley's 1784 *Sunday Service of the Methodists in North America* contained "The Order for the Administration of the Lord's Supper,"[7] which was a complete Service of Word and Table designed to be read from the book from start to finish. This did not meet the needs of the early American Methodists, and the more flexible pattern they adopted in 1792 provided that

---

7. *John Wesley's Sunday Service of the Methodists in North America,* with an introduction by James F. White. A Methodist Bicentennial Commemorative Reprint from Quarterly Review (Nashville: The United Methodist Publishing House and the United Methodist Board of Higher Education and Ministry, 1984), pp. 125 ff.

what we now call the Service of the Word be led by announcement rather than read out of a book. When Holy Communion was celebrated, the accustomed flexible, announcement-led pattern was followed through the Service of the Word; but Wesley's printed text was to be read for the Service of the Table (Holy Communion), starting with the Offertory.

Not having a printed text for the Service of the Word, but only for the Service of the Table, was the standard Methodist pattern until the Methodist Episcopal Church in 1932 restored the full Wesley Service of Word and Table in a considerably adapted form. Since then, many congregations have read this full service from their hymnals (Number 830 in *The Methodist Hymnal* of 1966). On the other hand, many congregations have continued to use a printed text only for the Service of the Table, and this has continued to be provided for (Number 832 in *The Methodist Hymnal* of 1966).

The Evangelical United Brethren brought a similarly mixed tradition into the union of 1968 which produced The United Methodist Church. Their last *Hymnal* (1957) contained both a full printed service of Word and Table and also provision for using the printed service only for the Service of the Table.

Meanwhile, although some congregations continue to be guided through services by announcement, many others in recent years have used bulletins. When they celebrate Holy Communion, their bulletins may refer the people to the Ritual in the hymnal, or they may put into their bulletins all that the people need in front of them for the whole service.

These four Services of Word and Table are intended to provide for all these diverse needs and traditions that are part of our denominational heritage. Each pastor and congregation is free to decide which of these services is most suitable and what adaptations may be called for.


# B. A SERVICE OF WORD AND TABLE I

This service is fully printed out in the hymnal, to meet the needs of congregations that wish to read the entire Service of

Word, as well as Holy Communion, directly from the hymnal, with as few choices to make and as few pages to turn as is possible. No bulletin is necessary, since such announcements as hymns and Scripture readings can be made orally or posted on hymn boards.

This service is also suited to special occasions where persons who do not worship together every week are celebrating Holy Communion without a bulletin and need a text that is largely pre-planned and easy to follow.

While this service will ordinarily be used on occasions when Holy Communion is being celebrated, it may also be used at services without Holy Communion where a text that can simply be read from the hymnal is desired. In that case, those acts of worship that pertain only to Holy Communion would, of course, be omitted.

In general, this service is best suited to congregations who worship most readily by reading texts and to situations where a specially printed bulletin is not feasible or desired. The suggestions given for each act of worship in chapter 4 ("An Order of Sunday Worship Using the Basic Pattern") apply to this service and to all the Services of Word and Table.

GREETING

The example given here illustrates the kind of clearly Christian greeting recommended in chapter 4. It is also an example of the call-and-response pattern that is so fundamental to our worship.

"The grace of the Lord Jesus Christ be with you," is the most common New Testament greeting. This is essentially the greeting that opens and closes the books of Romans (1:7; 16:20, 24), I Corinthians (1:3; 16:23), II Corinthians (1:2; 13:14), Galatians (1:3; 6:18), Ephesians (1:2; 6:24), Philippians (1:2; 4:23), Colossians (1:2; 4:18), I Thessalonians (1:1; 5:28), II Thessalonians (1:2; 3:18), I Timothy (1:2; 6:21), II Timothy (1:2; 4:22), Titus (1:4; 3:15), and Philemon (3, 25) and that closes the Bible (Rev. 22:21).

The people respond, "And also with you."

The leader then announces that "the risen Christ is with us." Christian worship is an encounter with the risen Christ, who as in the Emmaus story (Luke 24) has joined our gathering before we can even invoke his presence. This announcement is always appropriate, but especially so on the Lord's Day, when we celebrate our Lord's resurrection on the first day of the week and on which Christians since New Testament times have been accustomed to gather for a meeting with our risen Lord. It is even more appropriate when we have gathered to meet the risen Christ in the Lord's Supper.

The people's response is again simple and natural. "Praise the Lord." It is a fitting introduction to a hymn in which the people indeed praise the Lord. In other words, it (and the greeting as a whole) is a call, to which the hymn of praise is the response.

The two people's responses will quickly be memorized if they are regularly used. This will reduce the people's dependence on the printed text and make it possible for the leader to vary the first and third lines, if desired, from one service or season to another.

HYMN OF PRAISE

The number and perhaps the title or opening line of this and other hymns may be announced orally, posted on hymn boards, or printed in the bulletin. In making an oral announcement of this opening hymn of praise, the leader might build upon the last phrase of the greeting by saying, "Let us praise the Lord by singing hymn number —."

OPENING PRAYER

This classic "Collect for Purity," slightly modernized in its language, is suitable for use on any occasion. It was translated into English in the sixteenth century for *The Book of Common Prayer* from a Latin collect attributed to Saint Gregory, the eighth-century Abbot of Canterbury. It has come down to us through Wesley's 1784 *Sunday Service*. It should be prayed in unison by the congregation and is easily memorized. A prayer appropriate to the day, season, or occasion (such as Nos. 76, 201, 231, 253, 255, 259, 268, 281, 283, 284, 320, 321, 323, 335, 353, 542, 713, and 721) may also be used.

[ACT OF PRAISE]

Particular acts of praise are suggested in chapter 4 (pages 33-34). The brackets [] indicate, here and elsewhere, that this act can be omitted without doing violence to the integrity of the service.

## PRAYER FOR ILLUMINATION

This prayer, written by James F. White and revised by Fred D. Gealy for *The Sacrament of the Lord's Supper: An Alternate Text 1972*, was intended to be prayed in unison by the congregation. The prayer for illumination may take other forms, as described on pages 34-35.

## SCRIPTURE LESSON

The scripture lessons are announced orally. See the suggestions on pages 35-38.

[PSALM]  *May be sung or spoken.*

The psalm is also announced orally. See the suggestions on pages 37-38.

[SCRIPTURE LESSON]

## HYMN OR SONG

See the suggestions on page 38.

## GOSPEL LESSON

Two patterns of scripture readings interspersed with acts of praise are given here. The longer pattern consists of three lessons and two acts of praise. The shorter pattern, omitting what is in brackets [], consists of two lessons and a single act of praise. Both patterns illustrate the rhythm of call and response discussed on page 38 and elsewhere in this book.

SERMON

See the suggestions on pages 39-41.

RESPONSE TO THE WORD

Possible responses have been discussed on pages 41-43. The Apostles' Creed is printed here in the ecumenical translation. The traditional translation of the Apostles' Creed (No. 881), the Nicene Creed (No. 880), or an affirmation of faith (Nos. 883-889) may be used instead. These are described in chapter 11.

CONCERNS AND PRAYERS

The options here have been discussed on pages 43-46.

INVITATION

Since this service includes Holy Communion, the text of the invitation clearly indicates that not only confession and pardon but also Holy Communion are to follow.

The invitation text is adapted from the one written by James F. White for *The Sacrament of the Lord's Supper: An Alternate Text 1972.*

If an adaptation of this service is being used when Holy Communion is *not* to follow, another invitation should be used, such as this:

Christ our Lord calls all who love him
earnestly to repent of their sin
and live in peace with one another.
Therefore, let us confess our sin before God and one
    another.[8]

CONFESSION AND PARDON

This text is adapted from the prayer of confession written by Fred F. Gealy and the words of pardon written by H. Grady

8. *The Book of Services* (Nashville: The United Methodist Publishing House, 1985), p. 21.

Hardin and James F. White for *The Sacrament of the Lord's Supper: An Alternate Text 1972*. The words, "we have not loved you with our whole heart," were added by the 1988 General Conference.

When the people respond, "In the name of Jesus Christ, *you* are forgiven!" the leader should *not* join them, and the people by the way they say "you" should make it clear that it is addressed *to* the leader. This exchange between leader and people witnesses to our belief in the priesthood of the whole body of believers, not simply of the clergy. Then leader and people join together in giving "glory to God."

## THE PEACE

The peace has been discussed on pages 47-48 . An invitation to stand and other words of interpretation may informally be added to the sentence, "Let us offer one another signs of reconciliation and love."

## OFFERING

The introductory sentence specifically ties the offering in with the confession, pardon, and peace that have immediately preceded it. There may be congregational singing or choral or instrumental music as the offering is received. A hymn or anthem with a communion text is particularly appropriate (see the listing in No. 943 under "Holy Communion"). The bread and wine are brought by representatives of the people to the Lord's table with the monetary gifts, or uncovered if already in place. When the offering is brought forward and laid on the Lord's table, it is fitting that the people stand and that a doxology or other appropriate stanza be sung. No prayer is necessary as the money and bread and wine are being presented, since the Great Thanksgiving that immediately follows includes everything that needs to be said.

Following the Offering, a choice is offered: (1) the service may simply continue as printed; (2) a Great Thanksgiving other than that which follows here may be used, in which case the congregation should continue from this point with "A Service of

Word and Table III" (No. 15); or (3) if one of the musical settings of the Great Thanksgiving (Nos. 17-25) is to be used, the congregation should turn at this point to whichever setting they are to use and then may return to "A Service of Word and Table I" after the Great Thanksgiving.

## TAKING THE BREAD AND CUP

This is the first of the four actions of Holy Communion, based on the actions of Jesus in the Upper Room. Because Holy Communion is a meal, it is basically a series of actions and is more and more being understood as such. Holy Communion is far more than words, and it is significant that of its four actions only the Great Thanksgiving is primarily words. The other three are primarily nonverbal.

The pastor takes the bread and cup, which have been brought forward and uncovered, and does any necessary preparation of the bread and wine (grape juice). This is a very brief and simple action, done in silence; but exactly how it is done will depend upon circumstances.

Churches today are increasingly using a large uncut loaf of real bread, which later in the service is broken and distributed to the people. This follows the New Testament practice reported in I Corinthians 10:16-17. As Paul tells us, the one loaf powerfully symbolizes the fact that the congregation is one body in Christ. The loaf should *not* be broken at this time, since the breaking of the bread is an important action *following* the Great Thanksgiving. If the loaf is still wrapped or covered, however, the pastor should unwrap or uncover it at this time, before proceeding with the Great Thanksgiving.

If trays of wafers or bread cubes are used, either instead of or in addition to a loaf, the pastor should remove the lid(s) or covering at this time.

The symbol of a large cup, commonly called the "chalice," on the Lord's table is also powerful, even if the people are to be drinking from individual cups. If the wine (grape juice) is in a flagon or cruet rather than in the cup, the pastor should fill the cup at this time.

If trays of individual cups are used, either instead of or in addition to the chalice, the pastor should remove the lid(s) or covering at this time.

Since the late nineteenth century it has been customary in the great majority of United Methodist churches to use unfermented grape juice for the communion wine. While this is not a matter of church law, it is a practice that reflects pastoral concern for recovering alcoholics and respect for the consciences of total abstainers. Nonalcoholic wine is now also widely available and might be used.

## THE GREAT THANKSGIVING

As Jesus *gave thanks* (blessed) over the bread and cup, so does the pastor, ministering in Christ's name.

This prayer is a Christian version of the type of Jewish table blessing that Jesus undoubtedly used. In the New Testament, what was done is described both with the word *bless* (*eulogeo*, as in Matt. 14:19; 26:26; Mark 6:41; 8:7; 14:22; Luke 24:30; I Cor. 10:16) and with the words *give thanks* (*eucharisteo*, as in Matt. 15:36; 26:27; Mark 8:6; 14:23; Luke 22:17, 19; John 6:11, 23; I Cor. 11:24). In ancient Jewish tradition, the food and drink are blessed by blessing the name of God and recalling God's mighty acts.

The Great Thanksgiving likewise recalls God's mighty acts from a Christian perspective. It blesses God for the gifts of creation and redemption, recalls the origin and meaning of our actions at the Lord's table, and invokes the power of the Holy Spirit.

This was one great prayer in the early church, and it has now once again become one great prayer. In the Middle Ages the unity of this prayer was lost. It came to be regarded as several separate prayers, of which the chief was the Prayer of Consecration. This medieval fragmentation of the Great Thanksgiving continued until recent reforms, both denominationally and ecumenically, have restored its unity.

This prayer is led by an ordained minister or a local pastor authorized to administer Holy Communion (*The Book of*

*Discipline* 1988, Pars. 406 and 439.1*b*), but the congregation also participates in the prayer. The responses printed in bold-face type should be spoken or sung by the entire congregation.

On some occasions more than one ordained or authorized minister takes part in the service. It is the bishop's prerogative, when present, to lead the Great Thanksgiving and otherwise preside at the Lord's table, as well as to preach. In the bishop's absence, it is the district superintendent's prerogative, when present, to do the same. It is appropriate that other ordained ministers who are present be invited to stand with the presiding minister at the Lord's table. The Great Thanksgiving should not, however, be divided up between two or more clergy, as such a practice is not only awkward but makes the Great Thanksgiving seem like two or more separate prayers. Likewise, for two or more clergy to pray the Great Thanksgiving in unison is awkward and makes it more difficult for the congregation to hear and digest the rich content of the prayer. There are other acts of worship in the service that non-presiding clergy may lead, and they may assist in the giving of the bread and cup.

If the people are not already standing for the presentation of the offering, they should be invited to stand before the opening dialogue ("The Lord be with you. . . .") and remain standing throughout the whole of the Great Thanksgiving.

The ancient Christian practice was for the presiding minister to stand behind the Lord's table facing the people, so that pastor and people are gathered around the table; and increasingly this practice is being restored. For this reason, it is desirable that the Lord's table be free-standing, away from the wall, so that the pastor can stand behind it. If there is an altar table fixed to the wall that cannot be moved, a free-standing table may be set up to serve as the Lord's table. Suggestions for the design and placement of the Lord's table are found in the books *Church Architecture* (pp. 64-68) and *United Methodist Altars*, listed in the Bibliography.

The text of the Great Thanksgiving in this service is based on the most ancient Christian great thanksgivings and is for general use throughout the year. It is a positive, joyous thanksgiving for all God's mighty acts in Jesus Christ, particularly suitable as we commune with the risen Christ, on the Lord's Day or any other day.

## THE LORD'S PRAYER

By ancient tradition dating from the sixth century, the Great Thanksgiving is immediately followed by the Lord's Prayer, which should be prayed in unison by the congregation, standing. Musical settings are found in this hymnal as Nos. 270 and 271.

It forms a bridge between the first pair of actions in Holy Communion (thanksgiving) and the second pair (communion). It is both the sublime climax of our thanksgiving to God and the verbal entrance into a communion with God that is holy beyond words.

The people are called to pray the Lord's Prayer with the invitation: "And now, with the confidence of children of God, let us pray: . . . ." These words are appropriate because the Great Thanksgiving has just reminded the people of all God's mighty acts whereby they are God's beloved children, and because they are about to address God as Father in the Lord's Prayer.

The text printed in this service is the ecumenical translation of the Lord's Prayer, now used by many denominations in the English-speaking world. Since many congregations are accustomed to praying the Lord's Prayer in one of the two older translations used in the former Methodist and Evangelical United Brethren denominations respectively, all three translations are included in this hymnal (Nos. 894-896). Congregations wishing to use one of the traditional translations can simply do so from memory or turn to No. 895 or 896. On the other hand, congregations wishing to learn the ecumenical translation can do so by following the text in this service.

## BREAKING THE BREAD

The third of the four actions of Holy Communion, like the first, is brief and preliminary to the act that immediately follows.

Breaking the bread is a gesture of invitation to the people, done in the name of the living Christ, the Head of his family and the Host at this meal.

It should be done in such a way that persons immediately and intuitively perceive its meaning. Preferably, the pastor stands behind the Lord's table facing the people, lifts the unbroken loaf, and breaks it by hand. The loaf should not be partially pre-cut, since this weakens the symbolism of breaking it by hand. If it is necessary to use individual wafers or cubes of bread, one of the wafers (preferably a larger wafer) or a larger piece of the bread from which the cubes have been cut, should be broken. If the pastor cannot stand behind the Lord's table, the pastor should break the bread in such a way that the action is seen by the people.

After the bread has been broken, it is also a natural gesture of invitation to raise the cup while facing the people.

These acts may be done in silence, or while speaking the words from I Corinthians 10:16-17 printed in the text. These words, or others that might be used, express a part, but only a part, of the rich symbolism of these gestures. Our unity in Christ, justly distributing bread (all God's gifts) to the world, the breaking of Jesus' body on the cross and the pouring out of his blood, and the Emmaus appearance when the risen Christ was recognized "in the breaking of the bread"—these are but a few of the possible meanings.

## GIVING THE BREAD AND CUP

The fourth and last of the actions of Holy Communion, giving the bread and cup, has traditionally been called the "communion," a translation of the New Testament Greek word *koinonia* in I Corinthians 10:16, which can also be translated "participation," "sharing," or "fellowship." Each of these translations adds a new dimension to the meanings of *koinonia* and of the act of giving and receiving the bread and cup.

This sharing is primarily nonverbal—the giving of the bread and cup from one person, in the name of Christ, to another—but words are usually exchanged as the bread and cup are given and received. The words suggested in the text are brief enough to be spoken individually to each person being served; they should be spoken in a warm and personal manner, face to face. The touch of hand upon hand while serving adds to the warm and personal character of this holy *koinonia*. So does calling persons by name when serving them, although this should be done only if *everyone* can be called by name.

It is appropriate for the congregation to sing during the Communion, thus reinforcing the communal nature of the celebration. Hymns on Holy Communion (Nos. 612-641) are, of course, suitable; but these are not the only hymns and songs that are appropriate. It is generally good to use hymns, songs, and choruses that are familiar and beloved by the people, provided these are broadly appropriate to this holy occasion. The more people can sing from memory at a time like this, the better. A congregation that loves gospel songs, for instance, will find many songs and choruses that appropriately celebrate Jesus' warm and personal relationship to his people. Some congregations give opportunity for spontaneous song and praise. Large congregations where serving communion takes considerable time may wish to provide variety by interspersing congregational singing with appropriate choir, solo, or instrumental music.

The giving and receiving of the bread and cup can be done in various ways, depending on the size of the congregation and the design of the space in which they are worshiping.

Many congregations are accustomed to going forward in groups ("tables"), kneeling at the rail as a group, receiving the bread and cup from the pastor, and then being dismissed as a group. While many persons find this style meaningful, it can become an almost unbearably lengthy process when the congregation is large. To reduce the amount of time involved, additional clergy or laypersons can assist behind the rail in the serving of the bread and cup. Also, it takes less time if persons come and go freely at the rail, rather than being ushered to the rail by "tables."

Other congregations pass the bread and cup from hand to hand where they are seated. While this saves time, the serious disadvantage is that the people are denied the opportunity to be active—to come forward rather than to sit passively and wait. Where this pattern is followed, the people should be encouraged to make serving the persons next to them a personal gesture, perhaps exchanging words such as those given in the text. It is not necessary that all the people wait to eat or drink together at the same time.

An increasing number of congregations are finding that going forward, moving continuously past one or more places where the bread and cup are being given, and receiving communion standing combines the advantages of receiving kneeling or seated. In this way, the people experience communion as *active*—active coming to receive and active going forth to serve in the strength that communion gives. Persons may, if desired, be given the option of going to the rail immediately after receiving communion and kneeling there for as long as they wish.

At services, especially in small congregations, where the people can stand in a circle around the Lord's table or around the room, persons can easily and informally serve one another, with words exchanged as the Spirit moves.

However the bread and cup are distributed, this giving and receiving should be a clear and powerful acting out of the gospel. It is God's self-giving to us through another person. For this reason, one person should serve another. It is a powerful gesture when one person breaks the bread and places it in the hand of another person, or holds the chalice while another person dips the bread in it or drinks from it, or places an individual cup in the hand of another person. "Self-service" communion, where persons go to the table or to the rail and help themselves to the bread and cup, lacks the symbolism and power of this giving and receiving.

Likewise, the practice of having the place of worship open over a period of time for persons to enter and leave as they wish, to take the bread and cup without participating in the prayer and praise and *koinonia* of the church, destroys the communal nature of the service.

Whether the people receive the bread and cup standing, kneeling, or seated, it is quite appropriate for laypersons to assist in the giving of the bread and cup, provided the ordained or authorized minister clearly presides over the distribution. This is always done when the people receive the bread and cup seated. When the people receive kneeling at the rail, the person assisting the pastor may serve the cup to each person immediately after the pastor has served the bread to that person. Two or more pairs of persons may serve, each pair moving back and forth behind a designated segment of the rail. It generally works better for the pastor or the more experienced of the two to serve the bread. That person, in serving the bread, goes first and can make decisions regarding such matters as who may require special assistance, setting an example that the person serving the cup can then follow. When the people receive standing, those who serve likewise work in pairs, each pair receiving the bread and cup at the Lord's table and then going to stand at a designated "communion station," while the people pass in front of them and receive from them the bread and cup. In large congregations, any number of communion stations can be provided at various parts of the sanctuary, including any balconies or "overflow rooms." It is appropriate that laypersons chosen to assist in giving the bread and cup be carefully chosen and trained, and that this be seen by all as an honored ministry.

When individual cups are used, persons after receiving will need to do something with their empty cups. Congregations where the people receive seated in the pews commonly have provided racks for empty cups beside the hymnal racks in front of each pew; where these are not provided, trays may be passed again to collect the empty cups. Where the people receive kneeling, the rail is often designed so that empty cups may be placed on it; where this is not the case, a tray may be used to collect the empty cups. Where the people receive standing, a third person at each communion station may hold a tray for empty cups, or such trays can be set on stands, or persons may take them back to their pews and leave them in racks there.

Three questions continually arise with regard to our being inclusive in sharing the bread and cup.

1. It is our tradition to offer those present an open invitation to receive the bread and cup. One is *not* required to be a United

Methodist, and we have no tradition of refusing any persons who present themselves to receive. The text of the service, however, has made it quite clear that receiving communion is clearly an act of identification with Christ and the Church; and, for this reason, there may be persons present who choose not to receive. We should respect the consciences of such persons and do nothing to embarrass them.

2. Persons with handicapping conditions may require special sensitivity and consideration. Some require assistance in eating the bread and drinking from the cup. Others find it difficult if not impossible to kneel and may remain standing at the rail or seat themselves in the front row while others kneel. Others find it difficult to leave the place where they are seated. There are others who are sick or shut-in and to whom communion must be taken. Those severely handicapped in their mental capacities may not appear to us to understand what Holy Communion is all about, but may be communing with God in ways that go beyond our understanding. Well worked-out plans are needed for serving communion to all such persons, wherever and with whatever assistance may be necessary.

3. While congregations differ in their traditions regarding children receiving the bread and cup, an increasing number of congregations—both United Methodist and other denominations—are including them. When a child has received Holy Baptism, there is no biblical or theological reason for withholding from that child the other sacrament, Holy Communion. The children in a congregation are members of the family of Christ and, like all children, have a right to eat at the family table. A young child already knows the difference between being accepted and rejected at a meal and already connects being fed with being loved. Obviously there is much that a child does not understand about Holy Communion, but that can be said about all of us. The mystery of the gospel is revealed even to young children—perhaps *especially* to young children, if we remember Jesus' words: "Let the children come to me, and do not hinder them; for to such belongs the kingdom of God. Truly, I say to you, whoever does not receive the kingdom of God like a child shall not enter it" (Luke 18:16-17).

When all have received, the remaining bread and wine are returned to the Lord's table, and it is set in order.

What we do with the remaining bread and wine has a symbolic value that should not be underestimated. They may be set aside for distribution to the sick and others wishing communion but unable to attend. They may be reverently consumed by the pastor and others while the table is being set in order or following the service. They may be returned to earth—a biblical gesture of worship (II Sam. 23:16) and an ecological symbol today. The reverence that we show in our handling of Bibles may suggest what would be appropriate for the communion elements. Whatever we choose to do should express our stewardship of God's gifts and our respect for the holy purpose the bread and wine have served.

We have come to the end of the four actions that constitute Holy Communion, but it is natural to pause at this point for a brief prayer, thanking God for enabling us to share this holy meal and expressing the connection between our having received and our being sent to serve others as members of the body of Christ. The prayer, "Eternal God, we give you thanks . . ." serves this purpose. It was written specifically for this service, echoing an earlier responsive prayer written for *The Sacrament of the Lord's Supper: An Alternate Text 1972* by James F. White. It is appropriate that the people pray it in unison; but, if it would be awkward for them to return to the printed text at this point in the service, the pastor may offer the prayer and the people respond, "Amen."

HYMN OR SONG

See the discussion of the closing hymn or song on pages 52-53.

DISMISSAL WITH BLESSING

The first line dismisses the people in peace. The blessing that follows, commonly called the Apostolic Benediction, is from II Corinthians 13:14. It was *the* benediction recommended for American Methodists from 1824 to 1932 and has remained in common use ever since. The word "communion" is a translation of *koinonia* and has that word's wealth of meanings.

## GOING FORTH

See the discussion of the Going Forth on pages 53-54.

# C. A SERVICE OF WORD AND TABLE II

This service follows the tradition of Service of the Word (preaching service) in which the people are guided by a bulletin or by announcement, followed by a printed text that is used beginning with the invitation to the Lord's table. In many respects this service is like the Brief Form for Holy Communion in the former Methodist and Evangelical United Brethren Rituals and is especially suited to congregations familiar with that pattern.

The Service of the Word is outlined in a flexible pattern. *The people gather in the Lord's name. They offer prayer and praise. The Scriptures are read and preached. Responses of praise, faith, and prayer are offered.* See chapters 3 and 4 for further suggestions.

The service beginning with the invitation to the Lord's table is essentially the same as its equivalent in "A Service of Word and Table I," and the commentary given above for that service applies to this service as well.

In several respects, however, this service is shorter and more flexible than Service I.

THE GREAT THANKSGIVING is shorter than in Service I and can also be varied from time to time by adding, at some or all of the points marked with an asterisk (*), words appropriate to the day, season, or occasion. The adding of such words at these points will not be confusing to the people, because they are spoken only by the pastor and do not immediately precede any of the people's responses. This service can be used by the people while the pastor uses the book *Holy Communion* (Nashville: Abingdon Press, 1987) at the Lord's table. That book, designed for use by the pastor presiding at Holy Communion, includes eleven services of Holy Communion (Services 4 through 14) designed for particular days or seasons of the Christian year, all of which fit the text of the Great Thanksgiving in this service, filling in additional text at points marked (*). The pastor is, of course, also free to compose his or her own words for the day, season, or occasion.

THE LORD'S PRAYER does not include a printed text, leaving pastors and congregations free to choose the translation they prefer. (See Nos. 894-896 in the hymnal.)

BREAKING THE BREAD likewise does not include a printed text. If words are used with this action, they are chosen and spoken by the pastor and do not need to be printed for the people. The sentences used in Service I may be used. Also, a collection of sentences appropriate for this purpose is found in the book *Holy Communion* mentioned above.

After GIVING THE BREAD AND CUP, *the pastor or congregation may then give thanks after Communion*, but there is no printed prayer text. The pastor may choose or compose an appropriate prayer, such as the one used in Service I or one of the collection of prayers after communion found in the book *Holy Communion*. The pastor may pray this prayer, with the people responding "Amen," or may print it in the bulletin for the congregation to pray in unison or as a litany.

An alternative way of giving thanks after communion is for the final HYMN OR SONG to serve this purpose. Appropriate hymns or stanzas include "For the Bread, Which You Have Broken" (614 and 615), stanzas 4 and 5 of "Here, O My Lord, I See Thee" (623), "Now Let Us from This Table Rise" (634), stanza 5 of "You Satisfy the Hungry Heart" (629), stanza 3 of "Draw Us in the Spirit's Tether" (632), stanzas 3 to 5 or 4 and 5 of "I Come with Joy" (617), stanza 4 of "Come, Let Us Eat" (625), and "Father, We Thank You" (563 and 565). A more general hymn or song of thanksgiving, such as "Now Thank We All Our God" (102) or "Thank You, Lord" (84), may also serve this purpose. See also the hymns and stanzas listed under "Doxology" in the index (No. 951). If the congregation has been singing continuously while the bread and cup are given, and if there is no spoken prayer of thanksgiving after communion, this final hymn or song can simply be the last in the series of communion hymns.

## D. A SERVICE OF WORD AND TABLE III

This is the simplest and most flexible of the services of Holy Communion. Everything in the service except the Thanksgiving and Communion is guided by a bulletin or by announcement. Even in the Great Thanksgiving, there are only the "lead-in" or "cue" lines and the people's responses, which can quickly be memorized.

This service is designed to meet a variety of needs. It will appeal to people who prefer a style of worship that involves a minimum of reading. It will feel less "formal" to many people. It is also suited for congregations or situations that call for a high degree of variety and creativity. The more this service is used, the more familiar the "lead-in" lines and congregational responses will be, and the more "at home" the people will feel with it.

This Thanksgiving and Communion, for all its flexibility, follows the same pattern as in Services I and II. The commentary on the Thanksgiving and Communion given those services, and the commentary in chapters 3 and 4, apply here as well.

It is important that pastors who use this service carefully consider and prepare the content of the Great Thanksgiving. Since this prayer puts into words the Church's understanding both of God's mighty acts in Jesus Christ and of the meaning of Holy Communion, the one who leads this prayer is doing so as the authorized representative of the whole Church. This is at the heart of the meaning of ordination, and why the Church does not permit every Christian to lead this prayer.

A pastor preparing to lead this service might well begin by studying and reflecting on the Great Thanksgiving texts in

Services I and II. Indeed, one possibility when using Service III is for the pastor to read the Great Thanksgiving from Service I or II while the people have Service III in front of them. These are found in large print and easy-to-use format as Services 1 and 2 in the book *Holy Communion*.

Pastors wishing variety and creativity in the Great Thanksgiving are strongly urged to read and use *Holy Communion*. It was specifically designed to be used with Service III in the hymnal. Services 4 through 14 in *Holy Communion* are designed to be used with Service III for the various days and seasons of the Christian Year.

Pastors can go a step farther and print adaptations of Service III in their bulletins. "Lead-in" lines and the people's responses take far less space in the bulletin than does a whole Great Thanksgiving text. If computerized word processing is available, these "lead-in" lines and responses can be saved from service to service without retyping. Services 17 through 24 in *Holy Communion*, while they require modifying the Service III "lead-in" lines and responses in the hymnal, add new possibilities to the celebration of Holy Communion.

Pastors wishing to take another step and compose Great Thanksgivings themselves will find guidelines in the chapter of *Holy Communion* entitled "The Great Thanksgiving: Its Essential Elements."

Service III is also designed to be used when a Service of Christian Marriage or a Service of Death and Resurrection includes Holy Communion. Services 15 and 16 in *Holy Communion* are designed for the pastor's use when this is done. This is discussed more fully in chapters 6 and 7.

## E. THE GREAT THANKSGIVING: MUSICAL SETTINGS

So far, nothing has been said about singing the traditional communion responses. In the hymnal these responses are printed in a format designed to make using them easier and more effective than has ever before been the case in our hymnals.

The traditional communion responses are of two kinds: those outside of the Great Thanksgiving and those within the Great Thanksgiving.

1. Those outside the Great Thanksgiving are printed in this hymnal with the hymns, because this arrangement makes their use convenient and flexible. They can be announced or indicated by a line in the bulletin, just as is done with hymns. Since these are separate and distinct acts of worship, the service can appropriately come to a momentary pause before and after they are sung, just as happens with hymns.

"Lord, Have Mercy" (*Kyrie Eleison*) is found as Nos. 482, 483, 484, and 485. It is an ancient prayer response, originally in Greek, that can be used as a litany response in certain opening prayers such as the one on pages 35-36 of *The Book of Services*, or following the opening prayer (instead of, or just prior to, the "Glory Be to God on High"), or as a litany response during the concerns and prayers.

"Glory Be to God on High" (*Gloria in Excelsis*) is an ancient hymn that can be sung by the congregation (82), spoken with sung response by the congregation (83), or sung by the choir in various settings. It traditionally follows the opening prayer.

The Lord's Prayer is found in two musical settings (270 and 271).

2. Responses within the Great Thanksgiving include "Holy, Holy, Holy Lord" (the *Sanctus* and *Benedictus*), "Christ has died" (the Memorial Acclamation), and the Great Amen. These sung responses are printed as Nos. 17-25 within the outline of the Great Thanksgiving and with the "lead-in" lines that immediately precede them. By using this format, the people can pray and experience the Great Thanksgiving as a single, unified prayer without awkward pauses and page turns.

As with "A Service of Word and Table III," the pastor can take the full text of the Great Thanksgiving from any of several sources: "A Service of Word and Table" I or II, the book *Holy Communion*, or a prayer of the pastor's own selection or composition.

Five musical settings (A through E) are provided in order to meet the diverse needs of United Methodist congregations. Four of them are printed with only the melody line in the hymnal, since they should be sung in unison. Full accompaniment is found in the accompanist's edition of the hymnal.

Setting A, composed by Elise Eslinger, is very simple, joyous, and well suited to congregations just beginning to sing Communion responses. By echoing the familiar hymn "Holy, Holy, Holy!" and utilizing the most familiar musical intervals, it will immediately sound "familiar" and be memorized after being sung two or three times.

Setting B, composed by James A. Kriewald, is also simple and easily learned. Its call-and-response format enables the people, even on first hearing, to sing it without even referring to the printed page, simply by repeating what the leader has just sung.

Setting C, was adapted by Richard Proulx and Charles H. Webb from Franz Schubert's *Deutsche Messe* (German Mass). It will appeal because of its great beauty, especially when sung in the four-part harmony that is provided.

Setting D, composed by hymnal editor, Carlton R. Young, is the only one of these settings in a minor key. It is especially suited to more somber seasons and occasions such as Lent. It also offers interesting harmonies and rhythms.

Setting E, composed by William Mathias, is expansive and majestic. While it is more complex and demanding than simpler settings, it will richly repay the congregation willing to work at learning it.

In choosing which of these settings to use and preparing the congregation for its use, the pastor and those with musical responsibilities need to work closely together.

When one of these musical settings is used, the rest of the service can easily be printed in the bulletin. The "Thanksgiving and Communion" section of the bulletin might look like this:

TAKING OF THE BREAD AND CUP

THE GREAT THANKSGIVING—Musical Setting C Hymnal 20

THE LORD'S PRAYER

BREAKING THE BREAD

GIVING THE BREAD AND CUP

## F. A SERVICE OF WORD AND TABLE IV

This is a traditional text from the rituals of the former Methodist and Evangelical United Brethren churches. It can be used with a minimum of adjustment by those accustomed to using 830 or 832 in *The Book of Hymns* (*The Methodist Hymnal*) or the Ritual of Holy Communion in *The Hymnal* of the EUB Church. These services were all adapted from the service of Holy Communion in *The Book of Common Prayer* of the Church of England, which John Wesley sent to the American Methodists and which preserves the majestic sixteenth-century language style of Thomas Cranmer.

In both Methodist and EUB traditions, as we have seen, some congregations read the entire service from the hymnal, while others follow their accustomed Service of the Word (preaching service) by bulletin or announcement and then turn to the service in the hymnal for the Service of the Table. Both traditions are easily accommodated in "A Service of Word and Table IV," even though it does not include a full text for the Service of the Word.

The Service of the Word is flexibly outlined as follows: *The people gather in the Lord's name. They offer prayer and praise, which may include "Glory Be to God on High" (82). The Scriptures are read and preached. Responses of praise, faith, and prayer are offered.* This makes it clear that there is to be a Service of the Word, and that Word and Table should be experienced as a unified service. Holy Communion is *not* something "tacked on" to the Service of the Word, nor should it be a substitute for the reading and preaching of scripture.

It may be necessary to shorten the Service of the Word as compared with occasions when Holy Communion is not celebrated. In fact, a brief Service of the Word can be extremely effective. A short sermon can be just as powerful as a long one and should not be made light of by being called a "sermonette" or "meditation."

Those who wish their Service of the Word to include the familiar greeting, "Collect for Purity," and "Glory Be to God on

High" from *The Book of Hymns* 830 can easily do this by printing the following order in their bulletins.

GATHERING

GREETING
*Leader:* The Lord be with you.
*People:* **And with thy Spirit.**
*Leader:* Let us pray.

HYMN

OPENING PRAYER—in unison
**Almighty God, unto whom all hearts are open,**
**all desires known, and from whom no secrets are hid:**
**Cleanse the thoughts of our hearts**
**by the inspiration of thy Holy Spirit,**
**that we may perfectly love thee,**
**and worthily magnify thy holy name;**
**through Christ our Lord. Amen.**

ACT OF PRAISE—"Glory Be to God on High" Hymnal 82

SCRIPTURE

SERMON

RESPONSE TO THE WORD

CONCERNS AND PRAYERS

HOLY COMMUNION Hymnal 26

GOING FORTH

Congregations may wish to expand upon this order. For example, texts from "The Ritual of the Holy Communion" on pages 11 ff. of *The Hymnal* (EUB) may be included. The Scripture readings and acts of praise should be fully listed, as should all choir and instrumental music. Hymns, offering, affirmation of faith, and other desired acts of worship should be inserted in their customary place.

The musical setting of the "Glory Be to God on High" is the same as in *The Book of Hymns* 830. A full accompaniment is found in the accompanist's edition of the hymnal. The Gloria Patri (Nos. 70-71) may be substituted, as in *The Hymnal* (EUB).

As we move from the Service of the Word indicated by the rubrics to the text of the Service of the Table as printed in the hymnal, the invitation, confession, prayer for pardon, and words of assurance are taken directly from *The Book of Hymns* 830 and 832. See the discussion of these acts of worship on pages 46-47 above.

The exchange of the peace is optional. For a full discussion of the peace, see pages 47-48 above.

The placement and ceremony of the offering is flexible. For a discussion of options, see pages 48-49 above.

The biblical acts of taking the bread and cup and breaking the bread have been added to the service, without accompanying words. These acts do not lengthen the service and are fully explained above on pages 24, 62, 63, and 65-66.

The text of the Great Thanksgiving is taken directly from *The Book of Hymns* 830, with two brief additions from the Ritual of Holy Communion in *The Hymnal* of the EUB Church ("Blessed is he that cometh in the name of the Lord. Hosanna in the highest") ("Bless and sanctify with thy Word and Holy Spirit these thy gifts of bread and wine"). The musical setting of the "Holy, Holy, Holy" is the same as in *The Book of Hymns* 830; a full accompaniment is found in the accompanist's edition of the hymnal.

The prayer that in *The Book of Hymns* follows communion has been restored to its original position as the last part of the Great Thanksgiving. It is the natural completion of the thought in the prayer, which otherwise breaks off awkwardly so that it scarcely seems like a prayer. This restoration also has the practical advantage of freeing the people from having to turn again to their place in the hymnal after they receive communion.

For a full discussion of the pattern of the Holy Communion service, and of the Great Thanksgiving in particular, see pages 24 and 63-65 above.

The placement of the Lord's Prayer is left optional. Ecumenical practice, reflecting traditions dating back to the sixth century, places it following the Great Thanksgiving (see page 65). *The Book of Hymns* 830 and *The Hymnal* (EUB) place it after the opening "Collect for Purity." *The Book of Hymns* 832 does not indicate where it is to be placed.

The translation of the Lord's Prayer to be used is also optional. The ecumenical translation ("sins"), the former Methodist translation ("trespasses"), and the former EUB translation ("debts") are printed in the hymnal as Nos. 894-896. For a further discussion of these translations, see pages 203-204 below.

The Prayer of Humble Access is taken directly from *The Book of Hymns* 830 and 832.

"O Lamb of God" may be sung or spoken. The text and musical setting are taken directly from *The Book of Hymns* 830.

The words used at giving the bread and cup are taken directly from *The Book of Hymns* 830 and 832. The congregation sings hymns while the bread and cup are given. See pages 66-71 above for a full discussion of the serving of communion and the singing of communion hymns.

The closing part of the service after communion is left flexible; for a discussion of the options see pages 73-74 above. It is not necessary for the people to reopen their hymnals and find their place after they receive communion. Thanksgiving to God after communion is most appropriate; this may take the form of a prayer led by the pastor or printed in the bulletin, or a hymn or song, or both. The dismissal with blessing (benediction) is taken directly from *The Book of Hymns* 830.


## G. COMMUNION WITH THE SICK AND SHUT-IN

Since the earliest Christian times, communion has been brought to sick and shut-in persons unable to attend congregational worship. This is really an extension of congregational worship, and no discussion of Holy Communion is complete that ignores those who wish to commune but cannot unless it is brought to them. Sometimes the consecrated communion bread and wine are brought from the service to the sick and shut-in; in that case no further consecration is necessary. Sometimes other bread and wine must be used, and at least a minimum service of Word and Table is needed for their consecration. In either case, at least a brief service is needed to enable and express the communion of the sick and shut-in worshiper with Christ and the Church.

Such a service was officially adopted by the 1984 General Conference as part of the Ritual of The United Methodist Church. It is found on pages 31-33 of *The Book of Services*. Because it is not a congregational service, it was not included in the hymnal; but for the convenience of pastors who may not have *The Book of Services* it is printed here.

*The people come together and exchange greetings in the Lord's name. Scriptures are read and interpreted. Prayer and praise are offered. The pastor then gives this or some other suitable invitation:*

Christ our Lord invites to his table
  all who love him and seek to grow into his likeness.
Let us draw near with faith, make our humble confession,
  and prepare to receive this holy Sacrament.

*Pastor and people:*
**We do not presume to come to this your table, merciful Lord,**
  **trusting in our own goodness, but in your unfailing mercies.**
**We are not worthy that you should receive us,**
  **but give your word and we shall be healed,**
  **through Jesus Christ our Lord. Amen.**

*The pastor may say:*
Hear the good news: "Christ died for us while we were yet
  sinners; that is proof of God's love toward us."
In the name of Jesus Christ, you are forgiven!

*All may exchange signs and words of God's peace.*
*The pastor takes the bread and cup, prepares the bread and wine for the meal, and then prays the Great Thanksgiving as follows:*
Lift up your heart(s) and give thanks to the Lord our God.
Father Almighty, Creator of heaven and earth,

you made us in your image, to love and to be loved.
When we turned away, and our love failed,
    your love remained steadfast.
By the suffering, death, and resurrection
    of your only Son Jesus Christ
    you delivered us from slavery to sin and death
    and made with us a new covenant by water and the Spirit.
On the night in which he gave himself up for us
    he took bread, gave thanks to you, broke the bread,
    gave it to his disciples, and said:
"Take, eat; this is my body which is given for you.
Do this in remembrance of me."

When the supper was over he took the cup,
    gave thanks to you, gave it to his disciples, and said:
"Drink from this, all of you;
    this is my blood of the new covenant,
    poured out for you and for many for the forgiveness of sins.
Do this, as often as you drink it, in remembrance of me."

And so,
    in remembrance of these your mighty acts in Jesus Christ,
we offer ourselves in praise and thanksgiving
    as a holy and living sacrifice,
    in union with Christ's offering for us.

Pour out your Holy Spirit
    on us and on these gifts of bread and wine.
Make them be for us the body and blood of Christ,
that we may be for the world the body of Christ,
    redeemed by his blood.
By your Spirit make us one with Christ, one with each other,
    and one in ministry to all the world,
until Christ comes in final victory,
    and we feast at his heavenly banquet.

Through your Son Jesus Christ,
    with the Holy Spirit in your holy Church,
    all honor and glory is yours, Almighty Father,
    now and for ever. **Amen.**

And now, with the confidence of children of God, let us pray:

**Our Father in heaven, hallowed be your name,**
**your kingdom come, your will be done, on earth as in heaven.**
**Give us today our daily bread.**
**Forgive us our sins as we forgive those who sin against us.**
**Save us from the time of trial, and deliver us from evil.**
**For the kingdom, the power, and the glory are yours, now and**
**for ever. Amen.**

*The pastor breaks the bread.*

*The bread and wine are given to the people,*
*with these or other words being exchanged:*
The body of Christ, given for you. **Amen.**
The blood of Christ, given for you. **Amen.**

*When all have received, the Lord's table is put in order.*
*The pastor may then give thanks after communion.*
*A final hymn or song may be sung.*

*The pastor gives this final blessing:*

The grace of the Lord Jesus Christ,
and the love of God,
and the communion of the Holy Spirit
be with you all. **Amen.**

The above service should be interpreted very flexibly, depending upon the circumstances of the pastoral visit. "The people" may be simply the pastor and one other person. The service may be very informal and conversational. There should be every possible sensitivity to the particular needs of the person(s) receiving communion. While there should be whatever participation is feasible by the person(s) receiving communion, sometimes this may simply be gestures and expression. Any translation of the Lord's Prayer may be used.

Familiar acts of worship that persons may know by memory, such as the Apostles' Creed or the Twenty-third Psalm, may be used. Sometimes it is possible to sing one or more hymns. If the bread and wine come from a service in which they have already been consecrated, it is not necessary to pray the Great Thanksgiving, but a brief prayer of thanksgiving is appropriate.

# CHAPTER 6

# SERVICES OF THE BAPTISMAL COVENANT

## A. Introduction

Christians are a covenant people. The term "New Testament" means "New Covenant"—the covenant that God made and sealed with us in the saving work of Jesus Christ, and declared to us in baptism. This baptismal covenant is both God's word of grace to us and our responding commitment of faith. It is the foundation of the Christian life.

For those in the Wesleyan tradition, an understanding of the Christian life as a covenant is very familiar. John Wesley used the biblical idea of covenant-making as the basis for his service known to us as "An Order of Worship for Such as Would Enter into or Renew Their Covenant with God"—"John Wesley's Covenant Service." For this reason the title "The Baptismal Covenant" for the services of baptism, confirmation, and reaffirmation is a logical development within our United Methodist tradition, and at the same time is in line with the best ecumenical understandings and practice of Christian initiation.

There are five closely related services gathered together under the heading of "The Baptismal Covenant."

1. *Holy Baptism* is entrance into the covenant. It is the sacrament upon which all the other services of the baptismal covenant are based. While it is the same sacrament regardless of the age of the candidates or whether they can answer for themselves, it takes a slightly different form when candidates are children or others (such as the severely mentally handi-

capped) unable to answer for themselves. Infants and others unable to take the vows for themselves are presented by parents and/or sponsors. There may also be sponsors when candidates can speak for themselves. Since the vows taken by parents or sponsors are a personal Christian commitment as well as a pledge to nurture the candidate as a Christian, those who take them should be members of Christ's holy church.

2. *Confirmation* is the first public affirmation of the baptismal covenant by those baptized when they could not make the vows themselves. Those who are able to take the vows for themselves at their baptism are not confirmed, for they have made their public profession of faith at the font.

3. *Reaffirmation of Faith* is a public reaffirmation of the baptismal covenant by those who have already affirmed it in baptism or confirmation. Christians are encouraged to do this from time to time. This is often done when persons (a) join a congregation or (b) wish to testify to a particular experience of the renewing power of the Spirit in their lives. It also may be done by entire congregations on appropriate occasions such as the Baptism of the Lord (Sunday following January 6) or Easter. Such reaffirmation is not, however, to be understood as the Sacrament of Baptism. Baptism is not administered to any person more than once, for while our baptismal vows are less than reliable, God's promise to us in the sacrament is steadfast.

4. *Reception into The United Methodist Church* following baptism as an adult or confirmation, or when coming from another denomination. This is the act of joining our *denomination*.

5. *Reception into a Local Congregation* following baptism as an adult or confirmation or coming from any other Christian congregation is the act of joining *a particular local congregation.*

Persons often take more than one of these steps at once. Those being baptized as adults, for instance, are normally received at the same time into the denomination known as The United Methodist Church and also into a local congregation. Those joining a United Methodist congregation who have not previously been United Methodists are joining The United Methodist Church as well as that particular congregation.

When families or groups of persons are received, it often happens that all of these acts take place at one service.

One of the practical problems that pastors have faced has been doing all these acts as a unified service rather than as a group of separate and uncoordinated services.

The forms of service presented in the new hymnal makes it possible to do whatever needs to be done in one unified service. This unified service clearly establishes the relationship between baptism itself and the other acts that either accompany it or follow it in the course of a committed Christian life. It also decreases the length of the service in those cases where formerly more than one service would have been needed.

Careful planning of the service and discussion of the service in advance with the participants is a great help in preventing awkward moments and in making it meaningful for all concerned. It is a particular help to the pastor who is using one of these services for the first time to study the service carefully and go through it step by step, at least mentally if not in actual rehearsal.

In planning, it is important to notice some of the key sentences in the introduction "Concerning the Services of the Baptismal Covenant" (No. 32).

1. *Those within the covenant constitute the community we call the Church; therefore, the services of the baptismal covenant are conducted during the public worship of the congregation where the person's membership is to be held, except in very unusual circumstances.*

2. *These services are best placed in the order of worship as a response following the reading of Scripture and its exposition in the sermon.* This is more fully explained above on pages 41-43.

3. *In cases of emergency, the essential acts in baptism are the vows and the baptism with water in the name of the Father, and of the Son, and of the Holy Spirit.*

4. *A candidate baptized outside of a congregational worship service should, if possible, be presented at a later time to the congregation.*

## B. The Baptismal Covenant I

This service provides the services of Holy Baptism (both for those able and for those unable to take the vows for themselves),

Confirmation, Reaffirmation of Faith, Reception into The United Methodist Church, and Reception into a Local Congregation, or any combination of these that may be called for on a given occasion.

In this one unified service, for instance, it is possible, without duplicating any actions, to baptize an adult, to receive by transfer from another United Methodist congregation the spouse of that adult, to baptize their infant son, to confirm their teenage daughter, and to receive into membership the adult's parents, one of whom comes by transfer from another denomination and the other of whom is coming by reaffirmation of faith.

When a less complex situation presents itself, sections of the service may be omitted. The sections of the service have been numbered to make it easier to omit what is not applicable.

1. Perhaps the commonest situation occurs when only infants or others unable to answer for themselves are to be baptized. The Baptismal Covenant II (which omits sections 2, 6-7, and 12-15 of The Baptismal Covenant I) is designed for such situations and should be used instead of the Baptismal Covenant I.

2. When only those who can answer for themselves are to be baptized and received into the church, sections 2, 5, and 12 are omitted. Sections 7 and 13 *may* also be omitted.*

3. When there are only confirmations and no baptisms, sections 5 and 11 are omitted. Sections 7, 10, and 13 *may* also be omitted.*

4. When a confirmation class includes persons to be baptized, section 5 is omitted. Sections 7 and 13 *may* also be omitted.* Each candidate receives *either* Baptism with laying on of hands (11) *or* Confirmation (12), but not both.

5. When persons are being received into membership in a local congregation and wish to reaffirm their faith, sections 5 and 11 are omitted. If they are transferring from another United Methodist congregation, 14 is also omitted. Sections 7, 10, and 13 *may* also be omitted.*

---

*Section 7 is used only if there are sponsors.
*Section 10 is used only when there are baptisms or when water is to be administered as suggested in section 12 or 13.
*Section 13 is used only if the whole congregation is to reaffirm the faith in a service in which persons are being baptized, confirmed, or received.

6. When persons are being received into membership in a local congregation and are not reaffirming their faith, *only* sections 14-16 are used with those coming from another denomination, and *only* sections 15-16 are used with those transferring from another United Methodist congregation.

7. If the whole congregation is reaffirming the faith (renewing the Baptismal Covenant) and there are no individuals to be baptized, confirmed, or received into membership, the Baptismal Covenant IV should be used.

## C. The Baptismal Covenant II

This service is used when baptism is being administered only to children or others (such as the severely mentally handicapped) unable to answer for themselves, and when there are neither confirmations nor reception of members. It is the same as the Baptismal Covenant I, except that sections 2, 6-7, and 12-15 are omitted. When it is necessary further to shorten this service, at least sections 4-8 (the vows) and 11 (baptism with laying on of hands) are used.

It should be noted, however, that this service as it stands is shorter than it may seem. (1) In order to make the service easier to read and follow, more "white space" is on the pages and there are no block paragraphs. This format spreads this and every service in the hymnal out over more pages but does not lengthen the time they take. (2) Because the Apostles' Creed is a part of this order, an affirmation of faith will not occur at any other point in the service on that day. An unabridged oral reading of the new service will take about sixty to ninety seconds longer than the respective services of the former EUB and Methodist churches. This slight increase is entirely due to the important inclusion of the prayer of thanksgiving over the water.

## D. The Congregation's Pledge at Baptism I

The "Service of the Baptism of Infants" in *The Book of Ritual* of the Evangelical United Brethren Church is also approved for use.

The only act of congregational participation in this service is the pledge printed here in the hymnal. The rest of the service is not printed here, because it is needed only by the pastor.

## E. THE CONGREGATION'S PLEDGE AT BAPTISM II

"The Order for the Administration of the Sacrament of Baptism: Children" in *The Book of Hymns* (*The Methodist Hymnal*) 828 and *The Book of Worship for Church and Home* of The Methodist Church is also approved for use.

The only act of congregational participation in this service is the pledge printed here in the hymnal. The rest of the service is not printed here, because it is needed only by the pastor.

## F. THE BAPTISMAL COVENANT III

This service is a traditional text from the Ritual of the former Methodist Church and the former Evangelical United Brethren Church. It can be used with a minimum of adjustment by those accustomed to using 828 (Youth and Adult Baptism) or 829 ("Confirmation and Reception into the Church") in *The Book of Hymns* (*The Methodist Hymnal*) or The Baptism of Adults in *The Book of Ritual* of the EUB Church. It uses a traditional language style, while at the same time following a pattern similar to that of the other services of the baptismal covenant.

It is not suited for the baptism of children or others unable to answer for themselves.

It is also not suited for situations where the whole congregation is reaffirming the faith (renewing the baptismal covenant) and there are no individuals to be baptized, confirmed, or received into membership.

It may, however, be used for any or all of the other services of the baptismal covenant.

1. When persons who can answer for themselves are to be baptized and received into the church, the entire service is used.

2. When there are only confirmations and no baptisms, the prayer for those to be baptized and the baptism are omitted.

3. When a confirmation class includes persons to be baptized, the entire service is used, but only those who have not previously been baptized are baptized.

4. When persons are being received into membership in a local congregation and wish to reaffirm their faith, the prayer for those to be baptized and the baptism are omitted. The laying on of hands *may* also be omitted.

5. When persons are being received into membership in a local congregation from another denomination and are not reaffirming their faith, *only* the portion of the service beginning with the reception into The United Methodist Church is used.

6. When persons are transferring into a local congregation from another United Methodist congregation, *only* the portion of the service beginning with the reception into the local congregation is used.

## G. THE BAPTISMAL COVENANT IV

Although congregational reaffirmation of the baptismal covenant when there are to be no baptisms, confirmations, or receptions may seem new for United Methodists, it in fact has been in our heritage a long time. Many congregations have engaged in covenant renewal from time to time, using John Wesley's Covenant Service. The same theology undergirds both that service and the one presented here, but the Baptismal Covenant IV makes clear an assumption only hinted at in the Wesleyan covenant service—namely, that Christian covenant-making begins with baptism and that in one way or another all subsequent reaffirmation is baptismal in character.

This service is intended for occasional use at particular times of the year—during the Great Fifty Days that begin with Easter and conclude with Pentecost, during the time around New Year's and the Baptism of the Lord, during a series of evangelistic services, and on All Saints Day or Sunday. Of course, such special occasions of covenant renewal are especially effective if there are one or more baptisms, confirmations, and receptions; in that case the Baptismal Covenant I is used.

This service may also be used beyond the local congregation at events such as convocations and Annual Conference sessions.

It has particular appeal in ecumenical settings where communion together is not possible, but where all can unite in confessing their common baptismal faith.

Appropriate hymns for use in covenant renewal include 604, 606, 610, and 382-536.

While it is possible to conduct this covenant renewal without any symbolic use of water, the impact of the service is greatly diminished in such a case, particularly since the Thanksgiving over the Water is then deleted. In order to use water without in any way suggesting that this is rebaptism, see suggestions below on pages 105-6.

Careful interpretation of this service is necessary, particularly in congregations that have not experienced John Wesley's Covenant Service. Therefore, material is provided below that may be published in a congregational newsletter, included in a service bulletin, or announced to the congregation.

### 1. AN INTERPRETATION IF WATER IS TO BE SPRINKLED TOWARD A CONGREGATION

In baptism we were joined to God and to the whole Church of Jesus Christ through a gracious covenant. A covenant implies an interaction between parties. In the baptismal covenant God promises that we are adopted sons and daughters by divine goodness, not by anything we merit or can earn. In response, we promise to live as faithful people within the community of the Church.

God's promises are never broken. There is no such thing as rebaptism, because God never goes back on the promise to regard us graciously. But we continually break our promises to God, if only by forgetting about them. Therefore, we are called to renewal again and again. From time to time it is well for us to be reminded of our faithlessness and to reaffirm our part of the baptismal covenant.

Every time we witness someone else's baptism, confirmation, or reaffirmation of faith, we should renew our own commitment, whether aloud as a part of the service or quietly in our hearts. But on some occasions, even when there are no candidates for baptism, confirmation, or reaffirmation of faith, we can join in such a renewal as an entire congregation.

This is the meaning of our service today [*or other date*]. When we have reaffirmed our baptismal faith through the vows and the use of the Apostles' Creed, we give thanks over the water by recalling God's mighty works of goodness toward us and the whole creation.

In these actions we gratefully *remember* our baptism—not that we necessarily recall the event itself, but we remember the deep meaning of this covenant of grace. We remember God's mercy and strengthening power, and we remember our resolve to be faithful Christians.

As a way of reinforcing these memories, a bit of water is then used as a reminder of the water of our baptism. At this point the pastor will symbolically sprinkle water toward the congregation. Sprinkling is an ancient biblical action of renewal, as found for example in Ezekiel 36:25-26. There God says to the people who have forgotten the covenant God made with the children of Israel: "I will sprinkle clean water upon you, and you shall be clean. . . . A new heart I will give you, and a new spirit I will put within you."

There is no need for drops of water to touch everyone. This is not baptism but only a symbolic reminder of it. Yet in that act of sprinkling, recall all that God has done for you; and with thanksgiving in your heart, renew your commitment to Jesus Christ and his Church.

## 2. AN INTERPRETATION WHERE THERE ARE OTHER, OPTIONAL USES OF WATER

*For the final two paragraphs above, substitute this:*

Following the prayer, those who wish to do so are invited to come forward to the font. As a way of reinforcing your memory of baptism, you may use the water in one of several ways. Some may simply look at the water and pray silently. Others may wish to touch the water, or touch the water and then moisten their hands or faces with it as a reminder of God's cleansing and refreshing power. Still others will be familiar with, and comfortable with, the practice of dipping fingers into the water and then making the sign of the cross on the forehead—or on the forehead, abdomen, left shoulder, and right shoulder. Some members of the congregation may prefer to remain in their seats, meditating upon the covenant they have made with God. Regardless of your expression of faith, recall all that God has done for you, and with thanksgiving in your heart renew your commitment to Jesus Christ and his Church.

# H. The Service Step by Step

## INTRODUCTION TO THE SERVICE

The physical setting of baptism and other services of the baptismal covenant is important. Baptism takes place at a font or baptistry, which because of the importance of baptism should be in full view of the congregation every Sunday as a reminder of our baptismal covenant and should ideally have a prominence comparable to that of the Lord's table and the pulpit. Candidates and sponsors should come forward at the invitation and stand with the pastor as close to the font as possible. There should be enough space around the font to accommodate a group of candidates and their parents or sponsors, and there should be no barriers to block the access of the people to the font. Likewise, nothing should block the sight lines of the congregation. All need to see in order to participate.

A pitcher (sometimes called a ewer) containing water for baptism may be placed by the font throughout the service either every Sunday as a symbol that there is always an invitation to Christian discipleship, or on those Sundays when baptisms are expected—or, it may be brought forward to the font when the candidates and their parents or sponsors come forward, immediately before the Thanksgiving over the Water.

Congregations that use a paschal candle keep it lighted near the Lord's table from Easter through the day of Pentecost, then keep it beside the font the rest of the year, lighting it when there are baptisms.

The setting of baptism within the order of worship, following the Proclamation of the Word, symbolizes that baptism and other acts of commitment related to the baptismal covenant are *responses to God's initiative* as declared in the written and preached Word.

*As persons are coming forward, an appropriate hymn of baptism or confirmation may be sung.* See Nos. 604-611 and "Commitment" in the index (No. 939). Where baptisms are frequent, the congregation can learn a single stanza or chorus that can be sung regularly at this time.

The pastor makes an opening statement to the congregation (Section 1).

In Services I, II, and IV, the first paragraph of this statement uses biblical language drawn from John 3:5 and Isaiah 55:1 to set forth our basic understanding that although baptism is not to be confused with salvation, both are God's action and God's gift. Through the Sacrament of Baptism we are initiated into Christ's holy Church, just as through water and the Spirit we are given new birth and incorporated into God's mighty acts of salvation in Christ. This paragraph is used on all occasions.

In pre-baptismal instruction and preaching, and in the way the service itself is conducted, it is important to make a crucial distinction clear to everyone involved.

On the one hand, God's gift of baptism and the Baptismal Covenant include not only believers but their children (Acts 2:38-39). The New Testament records that believers were baptized with their households (Acts 16:15; 16:33; 18:8; I Cor. 1:16). Children are thus part of Christ's family, Christ's holy Church.

On the other hand, it is essential that these children, as the vow in Section 5 puts it, "be guided to accept God's grace for themselves, to profess their faith openly, and to lead a Christian life." The whole congregation, as well as the parent(s) and sponsor(s), undertake this solemn responsibility when a child is baptized. No candidate, parent, sponsor, or congregation should be led to imagine that baptism guarantees salvation and that faith in Christ will, therefore, be unnecessary.

The second paragraph (Section 2) reveals the relationship between baptism and confirmation. It is omitted when there is no confirmation or reaffirmation. Confirmation is a public affirmation by the candidate of the covenant made at baptism. For this reason, those baptized as youth or adults do not need confirmation, since their public affirmation is made at baptism.

In Service III the first paragraph sets forth the nature of the Church.

## PRESENTATION OF CANDIDATES

One or more of the forms of presentation are used as needed (Section 3). Presentation by the lay leader or some other member of the congregation is an indication that the Baptismal Covenant is common to all of Christ's people, not to the ordained alone.

The presentations may be informal and include a brief word about each candidate and their coming to this sacred moment.

## [PRAYER FOR THOSE TO BE BAPTIZED]

In Service III there is prayer for those to be baptized which is in some ways comparable to the Thanksgiving over the Water in Services I, II, and IV.

Some would prefer that the Thanksgiving over the Water be at this earlier point in the service (*before* rather than *after* the renunciation and profession of faith) in *all* Baptismal Covenant services. This would reinforce the understanding that God's grace comes before any action we can make in response, which has already been indicated by the prior reading and preaching of the Word. Ecumenically, baptism services are about equally divided as to whether the renunciation and profession or the Thanksgiving over the Water should come first. The pastor who wishes may reverse the order of these acts when using Service, I, II, or IV.

## RENUNCIATION OF SIN AND PROFESSION OF FAITH

Entrance into the covenant implies both a *turning from* sin and a *turning to* righteousness. Since the second century, vows implying both have been used in baptismal services.

*In Services I, II, and IV*, the first three vows (Section 4) move from the negative to the positive aspects of Christian commitment, drawing upon such biblical texts as Ephesians 4:22-24 and John 8:36. Following such biblical teachings as Ephesians 6:10-20, evil is set forth as cosmic, not merely individualistic. Further, the Church is shown to be a fellowship of people that transcends the barriers so familiar in our common experience.

Section 4 is used with all candidates for baptism, confirmation, and reaffirmation. Parents or other sponsors who take these vows on behalf of a child are affirming or reaffirming their own Christian commitment as the basis for the commitment they are about to make (in Section 5) to nurture the child as a Christian. Service I has a special significance and power on occasions when parent(s) and child(ren) are baptized as a family in the same service.

Section 5 is used *only* in the baptism of children and others not able to answer for themselves. One or more baptized and committed parents or other sponsors assume the obligations of Christian nurture by taking this vow. The use of one or more sponsors to take the vows *in addition to the parent(s)* is optional; it is especially common where there is a single parent. In unusual cases, other persons close to the candidate—grandparents, for example—may take the vows as sponsors *instead of the parent(s)* if the parents are unable or unwilling to make such a commitment themselves, but do not object to the Christian nurture of their child. Whatever the case, those who take these vows as sponsors assume a major responsibility and in no way should be regarded as having only an honor or courtesy bestowed upon them.

Section 6 is used in the baptism of those who can answer for themselves, but *not* in the baptism of children and others not able to answer for themselves. It is also used with candidates for confirmation or reaffirmation of faith. These persons promise faithfulness to the community of the Church and promise to be witnesses of Jesus Christ before the world.

Section 7 is included in the service *only* when some or all of those who have answered for themselves have sponsors. While we often associate sponsors only with the baptism of children, the practice may well be expanded. Youth or adults can choose—or have assigned to them—sponsors as a way of integrating them fully into the life of the congregation. New or immature Christians may find in such sponsors "elder brothers or sisters" or "mentors" in Christ.

In Section 8 the pastor addresses *the whole congregation.* Baptism is above all a congregational act. In addition to the sponsorship of parents and other individuals, the candidates need the sponsorship and nurturing care of the whole congregation. In these two vows, the congregation as the body of Christ reaffirms its commitment to Christ and makes its commitment to care for these new members.

But always the local congregation must be set in the context of the Church across the ages—"the holy catholic [universal] Church" whose faith the Apostles' Creed declares. Thus Section 9 consists of that creed, which appeared at least as far back as the third century as a statement of faith used in baptism and which has been widely used in baptisms ever since. Originally it was administered in the form that is here restored: three questions and three responses, declaring faith in the Trinity. The pastor puts the questions to the congregation (including the candidates), and the congregation responds. When the Apostles' Creed is used in this way, no other affirmation of faith should be included in the order of worship for that day. At any or every service of worship, use of the Apostles' Creed at the point in the order of worship where baptisms take place is a powerful reminder of the Church's faith, into which we were baptized and which we have professed.

Portions of the second and third response appear in brackets for disciplinary reasons. *The Book of Discipline* (Par. 211) requires profession of "faith in God, the Father Almighty, maker of heaven and earth, and in Jesus Christ his only Son, and in the Holy Spirit" but does not require profession of the whole Apostles' Creed. Because the Apostles' Creed is commonly used in our worship, however, and because it is a statement of the universal Church, unless candidates specifically decline to affirm more than church law requires, the entire creed should be used as suggested. Because many persons misunderstand the word "catholic," a footnote explains that it simply means "universal."

The ecumenical translation of the Apostles' Creed, which is used here, is discussed on page 200 below.

In Service III, which is used only with candidates able to answer for themselves, the renunciation of sin and profession of faith consists of the baptism and confirmation vows used in the former Methodist Church, including the whole Apostles' Creed with brackets as in Services, I, II, and IV. While use of the Apostles' Creed in baptism may seem "new" to many from the former Methodist Church, the former Evangelical United Brethren Church maintained the ancient tradition of using the Apostles' Creed in their baptismal ritual, as did the former Methodist Episcopal Church until 1932 and the Methodist Episcopal Church, South, until 1939.

Content of the entire service to this point makes clear the reason behind the introductory statement (No. 32) that normally "the services of the baptismal covenant are conducted during the public worship of the congregation where the person's membership is to be held"; for baptism is a corporate matter and requires the interaction of the newly received with the local congregation in faith and mission. Baptism is an act for and within the Christian family, not an individualistic act that can be done in isolation. Candidates become part of a congregation, which in turn is a part of the universal Church.

## THANKSGIVING OVER THE WATER

*If there are baptisms, or if water is to be used for reaffirmation, the water may be poured into the font at this time.*

(Section 10). To heighten the sign value of water, it is suggested that the font not be filled before the service begins, but rather that a pitcher or other large container of water be ceremonially poured into the font just before the prayer. This pouring is most effective when it is done in such a way that it is clearly seen and heard by the whole congregation.

Just as at Holy Communion the pastor at the Lord's table leads in a prayer of thanksgiving over the bread and cup, so at baptism the pastor, standing at the font, leads in a prayer of thanksgiving over the water. Over the water, just as over the bread and cup, thanksgiving for God's mighty acts is followed by petition for the blessings of the Holy Spirit.

We have every reason to be thankful for water and what it represents. Through water we are enabled to recall God's wonderful works—particularly the miracle of creation, in which life came forth from the waters of chaos; the Flood, in which Noah and his family were saved; the Exodus, when Moses and the people of Israel passed through the sea on their way to freedom; and above all the water of Jesus' birth and baptism. This thanksgiving leads naturally into petition for the blessings of the Holy Spirit in baptism.

Since ancient times, prayers of thanksgiving over the water at baptisms have incorporated these themes. John Wesley included such a prayer of thanksgiving in the baptism services that he sent to the American Methodists in 1784. Although American Methodists later shortened this prayer and removed from it the note of thanksgiving, a remnant of the petition is found in Service III as the Prayer for Those to Be Baptized.

In Services I, II, and IV the ancient and ecumenical Thanksgiving over the Water has been restored in a prayer that is concise, yet rich in biblical content. It quotes or recalls Genesis 1:2-3; I Peter 3:20; Genesis 9; Exodus 3; 14; Joshua 3:14-17; I Chronicles 16:23 (first response); Luke 1:31; 3:21-22; Mark 10:38; Matthew 28:19; I Chronicles 16:24 (second response); Mark 1:8 (Matt. 3:11; Luke 3:16); Acts 22:16; Revelation 7:9-14; Ephesians 6:14; I Corinthians 15:54-57; I Peter 5:6-11, concluding with a doxology (praise to the triune God). This prayer is the central expression in words of what baptism means, and to omit this prayer in order to save a minute greatly impoverishes the service. At three points in the prayer, the congregation is asked to join in spoken or sung response. Two musical settings are provided; No. 53 is simply sung by the people, while No. 54 is in a call-and-response style where a solo voice "lines" a phrase and the people repeat it. Both express the joyful nature of this congregational response.

## BAPTISM WITH LAYING ON OF HANDS

This act (Section 11) consists of three parts.

1. *Baptism proper.* In our tradition candidates may choose—or their parent(s) may choose for them—baptism by pouring, sprinkling, or immersion. The pastor pours or sprinkles water on each candidate's head or immerses each candidate in water, while calling the candidate by name and saying the ecumenically agreed-upon words from Matthew 28:19. Traditions vary as to whether this act is done once or three times, but the strongest weight of tradition favors its beings done three times—"in the name of the Father . . . , and of the Son . . . , and of the Holy Spirit." The people respond, "Amen."

In offering this choice of modes, we recognize that each mode of baptism brings out a part of the rich and diverse symbolism that the Bible links with baptism. Pouring, sprinkling, or immersion all suggest the *washing* away of sin (Acts 2:38; 22:16; I Cor. 6:11; Heb. 10:22; I Pet. 3:21). Being totally immersed (buried) in water and being raised from it symbolizes *burial and resurrection* with Christ (Rom. 6:3-5; Col. 2:12) and *being born* anew of water and the Spirit (John 3:3-5; Titus 3:5). Pouring or sprinkling water upon the candidate's head signifies God's *pouring out* of the Holy Spirit (Matt. 3:16; Mark 1:9-10; Luke 3:21-22; Acts 2:17; 19:1-7).

In any event, an ample quantity of water should be used, properly to signify the graciousness and generosity of God. When water is poured or sprinkled, the pastor dips the water up out of the font with the traditional shell, or a small pitcher, or a hand. Sometimes an acolyte holds a bowl to catch the water, or the candidate's head may be over the font itself. Towels are often used afterward.

In calling the candidate by name, it is traditional for the pastor to use only the given name(s)—the first name and the middle name(s) if any—without the family (last) name.

There has been controversy about the use of the masculine words "Father" and "Son" at baptism, and some have suggested alternative words. None of these alternatives is without serious problems, however; and ecumenical consultations indicate that baptisms using alternative words may not be recognized as valid in some denominations. General Conference explicitly rejected a proposal to adopt an alternative to the traditional formula. We urge that the traditional words be used at baptism.

2. *Laying on of hands*. Immediately after each candidate is baptized, the pastor places hands on that candidate's head and invokes the receiving of the Holy Spirit, in order that the candidate may be a faithful disciple of Jesus Christ.

It is desirable that laypersons, including baptized members of the family of the candidate, join the pastor in this action.

Laying on of hands is specifically linked with the receiving of the Holy Spirit in Acts 8:17-19 and 19:6 and is also mentioned in Acts 4:30; 5:12; 6:6 9:12, 17; 13:3; 19:11; 28:8; I Timothy 5:22; II Timothy 1:6. The laying on of hands in conjunction with prayer bears testimony to the way in which the community of faith shares, and thus preserves, what has been passed on from generation to generation of believers. It is the Holy Spirit who sustains this community, and therefore the prayer accompanying the gesture is for the work of the Spirit in the life of this new brother or sister in Christ.

Laying on of hands at baptism is new to some United Methodists, but it is actually the restoration of early church practice. For that matter, many United Methodist pastors have in practice combined baptism by sprinkling and the laying on of hands into one act, although these acts have much greater sign value if they are separate and distinct acts done one after the other.

When we notice the use of masculine language at the baptism proper, we may also notice in Services I and II, in the words used at the laying on of hands an instant after the baptismal words are used, a feminine and clearly biblical image of God as giving birth to Christians through water and the Spirit (John 3:3-8).

Different words are used with the laying on of hands in Service III. Some may feel that the use of the verb "confirm" here renders these words inappropriate for anything but a confirmation, but this is not necessarily the case. In laying on of hands following the baptism of a child, it is fitting that we pray that the Holy Spirit will, in the years to come, confirm that child in faith and fellowship. Following the baptism of those who have taken their own vows, this may be a reminder that they are receiving in their baptism with the laying on of hands everything that is given in confirmation. When persons reaffirm their faith, they will continue to need the confirming grace of the Holy Spirit. Pastors using Service III may, if they wish, use the words from Services I and II in the laying on of hands.

3. *Act of welcome.* In Services I and II, when all the candidates have been baptized, the pastor invites the congregation to welcome them. The words of welcome are rich in biblical content, recalling II Corinthians 5:17; I Peter 2:9; Galatians 3:27-28; Ephesians 4:4-6.

Several optional acts may be inserted immediately following the baptism with the laying on of hands and before the act of welcome. They should probably not be done, however, until the pastor and congregation feel comfortable with the service as it stands and are ready for something additional. In any event, the optional acts described below should not be emphasized so as to seem as important as, or more important than, God's sign given in the water itself.

The pastor may trace on the forehead of each newly baptized person the sign of the cross. This may be done in silence or with the words: "*Name*, [child of God], you are sealed by the Holy Spirit in baptism and marked as Christ's own forever." Olive oil may be used in this action, following the biblical custom of anointing prophets (I Kings 19:16), priests (Exod. 29:7), and kings (I Kings 1:39). Jesus' titles "Christ" and "Messiah" both mean "Anointed One," and the New Testament repeatedly calls Christ our High Priest and King. Christians in baptism "have put on Christ" (Gal. 3:27) and become members of the body of Christ (I Cor. 12:13), which is "a royal priesthood" (I Peter 2:9). Anointing at baptism is a reminder that *all* Christians, not just some special class of persons called "priests," are anointed into this royal priesthood. Incidentally, the word "christen" (meaning "baptize") literally means to "make Christian" and is ultimately derived from the New Testament word for "anoint."

New clothing is sometimes presented to those just baptized, particularly in the case of infants, as a symbol that we "have put on Christ" (Gal. 3:27) as one would put on new clothing. Such clothing is traditionally white, suggesting the "white robes" in Revelation 7:9-14. Words such as these may be used: "Receive these new clothes as a token of the new life that is given in Christ Jesus."

A lighted baptismal candle may also be presented to the newly baptized, with the use of such words as: "Let your light so shine that others, seeing your good works, may glorify your Father in heaven." The candle may be presented to the parents or sponsors of baptized children, in which case "others" may be changed to "this child" or "these children." It is appropriate to light the baptismal candle in the home each year on the anniversary of baptism as a reminder of the grace of God offered through baptism. A baptismal candle bears either a Christian symbol or no decoration at all; it should not be confused with ornate "birthday candles" sold commercially to mark off the child's birthdays. These candles may be lighted from the paschal candle (see pages 95-96), or from one of the candles on or near the Lord's table.

If more than one of these optional acts is used, it is suggested that they be done in the order given above.

## CONFIRMATION OR REAFFIRMATION OF FAITH

These acts (Section 12) have already been defined above on page 103.

*Here water may be used symbolically in ways that cannot be interpreted as baptism.*

As a means of emphasizing the relationship of confirmation or reaffirmation to the candidate's previous baptism, water may be used; the pastor may say, "Remember your baptism and be thankful"; and the candidate(s) and congregation may respond, "Amen."

This act is new to most United Methodists, and if it proves controversial it should not be done.

In any event, it is imperative that this act not in any way be confused with baptism or interpreted as rebaptism.

This act might, for instance, take the form of the pastor's touching the candidate's forehead with a moistened finger.

The words, "Remember your baptism," are not intended to mean, "Bring to mind your memory of the service where you were baptized." For those baptized in infancy, this would be impossible. Even with those who could remember the service where they were baptized, this interpretation misses the point. The meaning is: "Remember the meaning of your baptism—the gracious promises God made to you, the demands God placed upon you, and the need for continual response in faithful living." If "remember your baptism" is likely to be misunderstood, the pastor might say instead, "Remember that you have been baptized and be thankful."

*The pastor, and others if desired, place hands upon the head of each person being confirmed or reaffirming faith.*

The significance of the laying on of hands has already been discussed above. Unlike baptism, the laying on of hands can be repeated at key points in the life of a Christian to signify the continuing and growing work of the Holy Spirit. It is done at ordinations and at healing services, and also at confirmation and reaffirmation of faith. Notice the differences between the wording of the invocation of the Holy Spirit *in baptism* ("being born . . . be a faithful disciple") and *in confirmation or reaffirmation of faith* ("having been born . . . live as a faithful disciple"). After the pastor has invoked the Holy Spirit, the people respond, "Amen."

Section 13 is optional. *When there is a congregational reaffirmation of the baptismal covenant, water may be used symbolically in ways that cannot be interpreted as baptism, as the pastor says:* "Remember your baptism and be thankful," and the congregation responds, "Amen." This act, like the similar use of water with individuals described above, is new to most United Methodists, and if it proves controversial it should not be done. Again, it is imperative that this act not be confused with baptism or interpreted as rebaptism.

There are several ways in which this act might be done: (1) members of the congregation may be invited to touch the water; (2) the pastor may scoop a handful of water up and let it flow back into the font so that it is heard and seen; or (3) a very small amount of water may be sprinkled *toward* the congregation, not falling directly on their heads as would be the case in baptism by sprinkling. This may be done by dipping the end of a small evergreen branch in the font, or in a bowl of water carried from the font, and shaking it toward the congregation. This may be seen as representing biblical sprinkling with hyssop for purification (Exod. 12:22; Ps. 51:7) as well as recalling sprinkling as a sign of renewal in Ezekiel 36:25-26. Ways of interpreting this act to a congregation have been discussed above on pages 93-95.

## RECEPTION INTO THE UNITED METHODIST CHURCH

All those who have just been baptized as youth or adults, or been confirmed, or reaffirmed their faith now are received into full membership in The United Methodist Church (Section 14).

Persons coming from membership in other Christian denominations may have come forward previously and reaffirmed their faith, or they may come forward and be presented at this time for reception into membership in The United Methodist Church.

If there are no baptisms, confirmations, or reaffirmations of faith, all the preceding service may be omitted and a brief service receiving persons into The United Methodist Church and into a local congregation may begin here.

United Methodist congregations are part of a denomination, and members of these congregations are also members of The United Methodist Church who pledge to it and its ministries their loyalty and support.

Persons occasionally ask whether this means that United Methodists are pledging to remain in our denomination for the rest of their lives. Of course not! There are many situations where Christians may appropriately change denominations.

But it does mean that *as long as we are members of The United Methodist Church* we owe it our loyalty and support.

## RECEPTION INTO THE LOCAL CONGREGATION

All those who have just been received into The United Methodist Church are now received into full membership in a particular United Methodist congregation (Section 15).

Persons transferring their membership from other United Methodist congregations may have come forward previously, or they may come forward and be presented at this time for reception into membership in the local congregation.

If on a given occasion those being received into membership are all transferring from other United Methodist congregations, all the preceding service may be omitted, and a brief service of reception may begin here.

Service I includes a pledge to participate faithfully in the ministries of the local congregation.

In Service III those being received go directly to the commendation and welcome.

## COMMENDATION AND WELCOME

The pastor commends to the congregation's love and care all those persons who have taken any of the steps described above (Section 16).

The congregation then expresses its loving welcome and nurturing support and reaffirms its commitment as a Christian congregation.

The pastor then gives a blessing to those who have been baptized, confirmed, or received.

Either before (Service III) or after (Service I) these acts, one or more lay leaders or selected laypersons may join with the pastor in offering these persons acts of welcome and peace according to the customs of the congregation. One such act is "the right hand of fellowship" (Gal. 2:9).

The printed text should not be interpreted too rigidly to suggest that the service must be stiff and formal. Spontaneous words and gestures can give the service life and express the warmth of Christian love.

*Appropriate thanksgivings and intercessions for those who have participated in these acts should be included in the concerns and prayers that follow.*

*It is most fitting that the service continue with Holy Communion, in which the union of the new members with the body of Christ is most fully expressed. The new members may receive first.*

Because one of the highest privileges and chief means of grace is the reception of Holy Communion, it is most appropriate for the new members to share in the sacrament with the congregation on the day of their reception. As a mark of respect and hospitality, the pastor may invite these new members to receive the bread and cup before other members of the congregation.

CHAPTER 7

# THE UNITED METHODIST
# LITURGICAL PSALTER

## A. UNDERSTANDING THE PSALTER

The Book of Psalms was the Church's first hymnbook and serves still as the inspiration for more of our hymns than any other book of the Bible.

The Church inherited the practice of using psalms extensively in worship from Jewish temple ceremonies and synagogue services. Although many were written originally for use as private prayers, most were composed for use in the temple and were intended to be sung and accompanied by musical instruments. Trumpets, flutes, rams' horns, harps, lutes, cymbals, and drums are all mentioned in various places in Scripture as helping worshipers praise God.

Thus singing the psalms came naturally to the earliest Christians. The hymn that Jesus and his disciples sang after the Last Supper (Matt. 26:30 and Mark 14:26) was probably the second half of the Hallel—Psalms 115–118 sung in praise to God after the Passover. In Colossians 3:16 Christians are exhorted to "sing psalms and hymns and spiritual songs with thankfulness in your hearts to God." In Ephesians 5:18-19 Christians are urged to "be filled with the Spirit, addressing one another in psalms and hymns and spiritual songs, singing and making melody to the Lord with all your heart."

While Christians were not limited to the psalms in singing praise to God, the Book of Psalms was the Church's chief

110

hymnal through the centuries. During the first centuries it was apparently customary for psalms to be sung by a cantor (soloist) and a group. The group, depending in part on its level of ability, might repeat each verse after the cantor, finish each verse that the cantor opened, repeat the first verse as a refrain after each succeeding verse, or interject a short response after each of the cantor's verses. Later, when trained monastic choirs appeared, the two halves of the choir would sing antiphonally, each side taking one verse. Psalmody was heavily used throughout the entire liturgy of the Church.

The Protestant reformers not only retained this emphasis on psalmody, they extended it by teaching the people to sing psalms in their own language rather than in Latin. Martin Luther called the Psalms "the Bible in miniature." The metrical Psalter became standard in the sixteenth century with Anglicans and Calvinists.

Later, John and Charles Wesley learned to sing psalms as children in their household devotions, and throughout their lives they used them regularly in Sunday services and in Morning and Evening Prayer. Charles spent nearly four decades setting the Psalms in English metrical verse; and although these are not the hymns for which he is best known, they show his determination that the Psalms should continue to be sung.

For some years on the American frontier American Methodists largely lost this tradition, except for a few metrical psalms sung as hymns, but by the latter years of the nineteenth century, Methodists had begun to read psalms responsively in worship. The Psalter in responsive reading form became a standard feature of our hymnals in the twentieth century, and a few metrical psalms continued to be sung as hymns.

During the twentieth century the Psalms have been crucial in the lives of many Christians. The part played by the Psalms in strengthening the heroic life of Dietrich Bonhoeffer, for instance, is well known; and in his final tract from prison referred to the Psalms as "the prayerbook of the Bible."

At the same time, reaction to the responsive reading of psalms in worship has been very mixed. While many have found it meaningful, others have found responsive reading to be dull or uncongenial. *The Methodist Hymnal* editions of 1905, 1935, and 1966 each contained a quite different approach to responsive reading; and after a generation of use in each case, the committees preparing the next hymnal heard a mandate for change.

When the 1980 General Conference directed that preparatory work be done toward a new official hymn and worship book, it specifically called for "development, trial publication, and field testing, with suitable research, of a version of the Psalter suitable for United Methodist use."[9] This action reflected both widespread dissatisfaction with the existing Psalter among United Methodists and also a need to recover this biblical, liturgical, and devotional treasure, which has enriched Jewish and Christian worship for over two thousand years.

The Section on Worship of the General Board of Discipleship then set up a Psalter Task Force, which was active from 1980 to 1984. It was discovered that much had happened in other denominations regarding psalmody since the publication in 1966 of *The Book of Hymns*. Three national consultations on psalmody were held between 1980 and 1982, and the contemporary psalmody that was shared there aroused great enthusiasm. The Upper Room took an active interest and worked closely with the Task Force. A selection of psalmody was published as a special issue of *alive now!* in July/August 1981, and over 100,000 copies were circulated. In 1984 The Upper Room also published *The Psalms: A New Translation for Prayer and Worship* and *Psalms for Singing*, translated by Gary Chamberlain. Trial use of these resources produced many helpful comments and suggestions, which showed that there was a wide variety of needs and preferences among United Methodists regarding the Psalter and that much further work was needed to be done.

When the Hymnal Revision Committee began the task given to it by the 1984 General Conference, it set up a Psalter Subcommittee, which began to add its own creativity to the recovery of the Psalter that was taking place across the church and to the discoveries made by the previous Psalter Task Force.

---

9. *Daily Christian Advocate* of the 1980 General Conference, p. 476.

Hebrew scholars and experts in liturgy and music were added as consultants to the subcommittee. Members spent much time learning the various ways in which psalmody is now used in United Methodist churches both large and small. They also became more familiar with practices in Episcopal, Lutheran, and Roman Catholic congregations, with plans for a renewed emphasis on psalm singing in Presbyterian churches, and with the singing of Scripture songs in many evangelical and pentecostal congregations. They considered how psalmody could most effectively be renewed in a denomination such as ours.

A major decision early in the process was the selection of the basic text for the Psalter. Existing translations of the Psalms were evaluated for their faithfulness to the Hebrew text and format, their readability, their effectiveness when read aloud, their familiarity to United Methodists, and their adaptability to more inclusive language possibilities. Standard translations by recognized groups of scholars, versions in other denominational psalters, and new translations by individuals were read aloud in committee meetings as part of this selection process. When the subcommittee learned that a new Revised Standard Version of the Bible was being prepared, they procured and studied advance copies of its Book of Psalms and after careful consideration chose it as the basic text for the new United Methodist Psalter.

Although the new RSV translation moves toward inclusive language, it does not go far enough to be consistent with the rest of the new hymnal. Therefore, a special Psalm Text Committee was formed to work on the creation of a United Methodist Liturgical Psalter that would be based on the new Revised Standard Version but not follow it strictly. The members were Professor Harrell F. Beck (since deceased) of Boston University School of Theology; Professor John C. Holbert of Perkins School of Theology; Dr. S T Kimbrough, Jr., of the Center for Theological Inquiry at Princeton; and the Reverend Alan Luff, Precentor at Westminster Abbey in London. They developed the following guidelines, which were in turn adopted by the Hymnal Revision Committee.

The work on the United Methodist Liturgical Psalter reflects the principles set forth in the inclusive language guidelines adopted by the Hymnal Revision Committee integrated with a serious regard for the integrity of the Hebrew text.

1. As a general rule, the English neuter is used for inanimate objects regardless of the Hebrew gender. See Psalm 46:5.

2. The third-person masculine singular is retained when translating the third-person masculine singular Hebrew pronoun that refers to the psalmist. See Psalms 2:28; 41:5, 8.

3. The third-person singular generic nouns and pronouns usually are rendered in the plural. See Psalms 1:1; 8:4; 14:6.

4. When third-person masculine singular Hebrew pronouns appear as a suffix or in a prepositional phrase referring to God and the antecedent is clear, the pronouns are rendered by the definite article or the demonstrative pronoun. [Note: This was modified by General Conference action; see below.] When rendering the text for inclusive language purposes would require paraphrasing and/or alteration of the Hebrew text or parallelism, the language of the new Revised Standard Version usually is retained.

5. When the word *melek* (king) refers to God metaphorically, it is translated "Ruler." When an earthly ruler is intended, it is translated "king." In the following instances it has been translated "Ruler": Psalms 44:4; 47:2, 6, 7; 48:2; 84:3; 95:3; 98:6; 99:4.

6. In North American language usage, the words for "Lord" and "God" are essentially synonymous; therefore, they have been used interchangeably in the Psalter Task Force's work.

Dr. Kimbrough has written further concerning the sixth guideline:

The new Revised Standard Version consistently translates YHWH as "Lord" and *'Elohim* as "God." The Psalter Text Committee has had as a primary concern faithfulness to the biblical text so that the United Methodist Liturgical Psalter has integrity as a translation. It is important to recognize that for the first time in the history of American Protestantism a major denomination is preparing a liturgical Psalter for public worship based upon a primary biblical translation (which already has wide acceptance in United Methodism) with a genuine concern for the meaning of the text, readability, singability, and inclusive language.

One cannot be faithful to the biblical text and render the two primary names for God (YHWH and *'Elohim*) by one name only, e.g., "God." While *'Elohim* can be a synonym for YHWH, the reverse is not necessarily the case, for YHWH embodies nuances of meaning not found in *'Elohim*. As in the case of the new Revised Standard Version, when the divine name YHWH appears in the psalm texts, it is rendered "Lord" in the United Methodist Liturgical Psalter. . . .

The interchangeable use of the words "Lord" and "God" has made it possible to provide a text that is faithful to the biblical text as a translation and which allows the text to speak of God in the third-person singular, as it does, without referring to God with third-person masculine singular pronouns. In producing a text for public reading which flows with understandability and which is faithful to Hebrew poetry and reflects effective assonance and alliteration, the opinion to use these names of God interchangeably was the enabling factor for retaining the third-person singular in reference to God without an exclusive male reference. . . .

There is no question that the biblical text of the psalms does refer to God with the third-person masculine singular pronoun; however, it is erroneous to assume that the authors of the psalms wanted thereby to impute explicit masculinity to God. For example, just because the word "girl," *Maedchen*, in the German language is neuter by no means suggests that the German language understands girls to be genderless. Here one encounters a philological characteristic of a language which must be understood from within the language.

By retaining the word "Lord" as a name for God and allowing it to stand in the third-person singular without dependence on the masculine gender one reclaims that word in the spirit of the Hebrew scriptures in referring to the God YHWH to whom all creation owes full allegiance in life and in death.

The 1988 General Conference in adopting this Psalter modified these guidelines by restoring the pronoun "his" with reference to God in about 30 percent of the psalms. The translation of these verses as originally proposed was as follows:

*Psalm 3:4*    I cry aloud to the Lord
               who answers me from the holy hill.
*Psalm 22:31*  and proclaim deliverance to a people yet unborn,
               that the Lord has wrought it.
*Psalm 27:5*   The Lord will hide me in a shelter

in the day of trouble,
will conceal me under the cover of the Lord's tent,
and will set me high upon a rock.

*Psalm 28:8* The Lord is the strength of the people,
the saving refuge of the anointed.

*Psalm 29:2* Ascribe to the Lord a glorious name;
worship the Lord in holy splendor.

*Psalm 29:9* The voice of the Lord makes the oaks to whirl,
and strips the forests bare;
and in the temple all cry, "Glory!"

*Psalm 29:11* May the Lord give strength to the people!
May the Lord bless the people with peace!

*Psalm 30:4* Sing praises to the Lord, O you saints,
and give thanks to God's holy name.

*Psalm 34:9* O fear the Lord, you holy ones,
for those who fear God have no want!

*Psalm 34:22* The Lord redeems the life of the servants;
none of those who take refuge in God
will be condemned.

*Psalm 42:8* By day the Lord commands steadfast love;
and at night God's song is with me,
a prayer to the God of my life.

*Psalm 47:8* God reigns over the nations;
God sits on the holy throne.

*Psalm 66:20* Blessed be God,
who has not rejected my prayer
or removed steadfast love from me.

*Psalm 78:32* They did not believe in these wonders,

*Psalm 85:8* Let me hear what God will speak
for the Lord will speak peace to the people,
to the saints, to those who turn to the Lord
in their hearts.

*Psalm 91:4a* and will cover you with pinions;

*Psalm 91:11* For God will give angels charge over you
to guard you in all your ways.

*Psalm 96:13b* The Lord will judge the world with righteousness,
and the peoples with truth.

*Psalm 97:3*       Fire goes before the Lord,
          and burns up the adversaries round about.

*Psalm 97:10*     The Lord loves those who hate evil,
          preserves the lives of the saints,
          and delivers them from the hand of the wicked.

*Psalm 98:2*       The Lord has declared victory,
          and has revealed vindication
            in the sight of the nations.

*Psalm 98:3a*     The Lord has remembered steadfast love
          and faithfulness
          to the house of Israel.

*Psalm 99:9*       Extol the Lord our God,
          and worship at the holy mountain;
          for the Lord our God is holy!

*Psalm 102:16*    For the Lord will build up Zion,
          and will appear in glory;

*Psalm 102:19a*   that the Lord looked down from the holy height,

*Psalm 103:18*    to those who keep the covenant
          and remember to do God's commandments.

*Psalm 104:31*    May the glory of the Lord endure forever,
          may the Lord rejoice in these works.

*Psalm 105:4a*   Seek the Lord and be strengthened,

*Psalm 105:8*     The Lord is mindful of the everlasting covenant,
          of the word commanded for a thousand
            generations,

*Psalm 105:9*     the covenant made with Abraham,
          the promise sworn to Isaac,

*Psalm 106:8a*   God saved them for the sake of the holy name,

*Psalm 106:23*    Therefore the Lord intended to destroy them
          had not Moses, the chosen one,
          stood in the breach,
          to turn away God's wrath from destroying them.

*Psalm 107:8*     Let them thank the Lord for steadfast love,
          for wonderful works to humankind.

*Psalm 111:4*     who has caused these wonderful works to be
          remembered; the Lord is gracious and merciful.

*Psalm 111:5*     The Lord provides food for those who are faithful
          and is ever mindful of the covenant.

| | |
|---|---|
| *Psalm 111:6a* | The Lord has shown the power of these works, to God's people, |
| *Psalm 111:9a* | The Lord sent redemption to this people; |
| *Psalm 116:2* | and has inclined an ear to me whenever I called. |
| *Psalm 116:14,18* | I will pay my vows to the Lord in the presence of all the people. |
| *Psalm 116:15* | Precious in the sight of the Lord is the death of the saints. |
| *Psalm 135:14* | For the Lord will vindicate this people, and have compassion on these faithful servants. |
| *Psalm 145:9* | The Lord is good to all, compassionate over all creation. |
| *Psalm 148:2* | Praise the Lord, all angels, praise the Lord, all hosts! |
| *Psalm 148:14a* | God has raised up a horn for the people, praise for all the saints, |
| *Psalm 150:1* | Praise the Lord! Praise God in the sanctuary; praise God in the mighty firmament! |
| *Psalm 150:2* | Praise God for mighty deeds; praise God for exceeding greatness! |

The familiar King James or Coverdale versions of Psalms 23 (137), 24 (212), 100 (74), and 130 (516) are in the hymns section of the new hymnal, in addition to being in the Psalter in the new translation. Psalm 23 in the King James Version and an adaptation of the King James Version of Psalm 130 are also included in the Service of Death and Resurrection (873).

Another important decision was the number of psalms that should be included and the way they should be selected. The Psalter Subcommittee began with the 111 psalms or psalm portions in the 1983 Common Lectionary. The final Psalter includes 100 complete or partial psalms.

Six psalms that were not in the Common Lectionary were included. Psalm 39 is a lament to balance the lectionary's emphasis on praise and thanksgiving. Psalm 134 is especially good in Evening Praise and Prayer. Psalm 148 served as the inspiration for Francis of Assisi's "Canticle of the Sun," known to us as the hymn "All Creatures of Our God and King" (62).

Fourteen psalms found in the 1983 Common Lectionary are omitted from the United Methodist Liturgical Psalter. Those using the Common Lectionary can readily make the following substitutions:

| Omitted | Recommended Substitute |
|---------|------------------------|
| 20 | 72 |
| 21 | 72 |
| 26 | 25 or 28 |
| 35 | 25 or 28 |
| 45 | 72 or 100 |
| 53 | 14 |
| 57 | 63 |
| 69 | 63 |
| 94 | 63 |
| 101 | 99 |
| 125 | 124 or 126 |
| 127 | 42 |
| 128 | 95 |
| 149 | 148 or 150 |

The following canticles (songs from Scripture or Apocrypha other than psalms) are included with the hymns:

Exodus 15:1-6, 11-13, 17-18, 20-21 (135) Song of Moses and Miriam
Isaiah 55:6-11 (125) Canticle of Covenant Faithfulness
Luke 1:46b-55 (199) Canticle of Mary (*Magnificat*)
Luke 1:68-79 (208) Canticle of Zechariah (*Benedictus*)
Luke 2:29-32 (225) Canticle of Simeon (*Nunc Dimittis*)
Philippians 2:5-11 (167) Canticle of Christ's Obedience
Psalms 95:1-7; 96:9, 13 (91) Canticle of Praise to God (*Venite*)
Isaiah 9:2; 59:9-10; Psalm 139:11-12; Daniel 2:20, 22; I John 1:5 (205) Canticle of Light and Darkness

John 5:12; Ephesians 5:30-31; Psalm 34:8; 127:1; Song of Solomon 6:6;
    8:7; Romans 2:9; 12:16; I Corinthians 13:4-8; Colossians 3:12, 14;
    I John 3:18; Tobit 8:7 (646) Canticle of Love
Revelation 21:1-6, 23-24; 22:5, 12, 20 (734) Canticle of Hope
Wisdom of Solomon 3:1-9 (652) Canticle of Remembrance
Wisdom of Solomon 7:15, 24-30 (112) Canticle of Wisdom

The same guidelines were applied to these texts as were applied
to the Psalms, so as to give continuity throughout the hymnal to
sung Scripture. Some of these canticles are traditionally used for
Sunday worship or for morning or evening prayer, and new
canticles have been created for weddings and funerals.

Further decisions were needed regarding the liturgical form
and uses of the Psalter. While some United Methodist churches
have moved to singing the Psalms, most still speak them as
responsive readings. Many United Methodists will probably
continue to prefer responsive reading. On the other hand,
singing rather than merely speaking the psalms is crucial in
recovering the power of the Psalms. Therefore, the United
Methodist Liturgical Psalter takes a form that permits reading,
singing, or a combination of reading and singing.

There is at least one response to be sung or said with each psalm.
These responses can bring new life to the use of psalms in worship.
For the first time, a major denominational hymnal has a Psalter in
which every psalm has at least one response that the congregation
can either sing or speak to enhance the power of the psalm. The
words of these responses are from the Psalms, accompanying
lectionary texts, other biblical texts, and texts from outside the Bible
such as the words of familiar hymns. Most of these responses are
set to music composed for this specific purpose. Often fragments
from familiar, appropriate hymns have been selected. In all cases,
the text and tune of the response have been matched with the
particular psalm and consideration given to the mood of the psalm
and the season of the church year.

## B. USING THE PSALTER

This Psalter has been designed to be used in a variety of ways.
What is effective in one local church or on one occasion may not

work in another. If a new way of using the Psalter is being introduced, it is important to prepare the people so that they are not confused and can quickly learn to experience the new way as effective worship.

However the Psalter is used, both its place in our worship and its internal structure are best understood in the light of the call-and-response pattern, which is basic in our worship and is itself imitative of God's call to us and our response.

The place of the Psalter in an order of worship is normally as a response of praise following a call such as the reading of Scripture. God has called us through the reading of the Word, and we are responding to God with praise. Standing, which is appropriate for praise, is generally appropriate when using the Psalter as praise.

There are, however, exceptions. If a psalm is being read as a scripture lesson rather than as an act of praise, as for instance if the sermon is to be based on that psalm, then it becomes primarily call rather than response. It may then be appropriate for the congregation to read the psalm in unison, without using the response, while seated as a posture for receiving God's teaching. On the other hand, the other ways of using the Psalter discussed below may be appropriate here as well, and standing here may be appropriate in the light of the way in which the Psalms make us feel in direct dialogue with God.

The internal structure of each psalm in this Psalter also shows a call-and-response pattern.

First, the verses of the psalm itself are printed in alternating light and boldface type. Previous hymnals have accustomed United Methodists to this "responsive reading" format. The leader may read the light type and the congregation the boldface type, or one side of the congregation may read the light type and the other side the boldface type.

Second, at least one response that can be sung or spoken is now provided for each psalm, like a chorus or refrain. Look at Psalm 1 (738) as an example. Just after the word "Response" printed in red are the words "Easter and General" in parentheses. This means that the first response is appropriate for the Easter Season or for any Sunday. The small printing at the upper right just above the music indicates that the text for the response comes from Psalm 1, verses 1*b* and 2*a*. Immediately below the text source the name of the composer is listed. A second response is printed below the first as an alternative to the first response. The letter "R" is printed in red three times—at the beginning of the psalm, after verse 3, and at the end of the psalm—indicating that one of the above responses may be sung or spoken at these three points in the psalm.

The format of the Psalter is also the format of the canticles printed among the hymns. These canticles can be used in the same variety of ways as can the Psalter.

This flexible format gives United Methodists a wide choice of ways to use the Psalter and canticles in worship.

1. The verses may be read in the familiar responsive reading fashion, the leader reading the light type and the congregation the boldface type, omitting the response at the top of the page.

2. The congregation may read the verses in unison, omitting the response at the top of the page. This tends to make the psalm or canticle a Scripture reading rather than an act of praise and might be appropriate if it is to be the text for the sermon or if the particular psalm (such as Psalm 8) lends itself to unison reading.

3. The two sides of the congregation may read the verses antiphonally, omitting the response at the top of the page. Those on the congregation's left (leader's right) may read the light type, and those on the other side the boldface type. Many congregations have found this to be more effective than leader-congregation responsive reading. The dividing point may be a center aisle or an imaginary center point in a center section of seating. The leader may lead both sides of the congregation, although some congregations find they need leadership chiefly to get started and need very little thereafter.

4. The verses may be read in any of the above ways, with the response being spoken in unison by everyone at the points indicated by a red "R."

5. The verses may be read in any of the above ways, with the response being sung by everyone at the points indicated by the red "R." The accompanist's edition of the hymnal has the full music for each response, while the pew edition has only the

melody line that the people are to sing. The leader (or solo voice, or choir) sings the response, then the congregation repeats it. Then as the verses are read, the congregation sings the response wherever a red "R" occurs. When the response is sung in the middle, or at the end, of the verses, the accompanist plays only a single-chord introduction (or the small-note introduction provided by the composer), with the congregation then immediately singing the response. If the small notes at the beginning of the response are in parentheses, as in Psalm 3, it means that they are *not* to be played when the whole response is played through as an introduction at the beginning of the service, but *are* to be played at other times.

6. A "cantor" (soloist) may sing the verses, using the instructions and psalm tones found in the hymnal No. 737, with the congregation singing the response as in (5). Only the cantor and accompanist need to be familiar with the instructions found on that page. Note that the key in which the psalm tone is to be sung will have to be adapted to the key of the response. Later it may be possible to train the choir or even the whole congregation to sing psalm tones, so that they can sing the verses in leader-people, left-right, or unison style. If preferred, even the response may be sung to the psalm tone rather than to the printed tune.

7. One of the many hymns that are metrical psalms or whose words are based on Psalms may be used as the psalm from time to time. These are listed under "Psalms" in the Index of Scripture (Nos. 924-925).

Teaching a congregation to sing the response, as in (5) and (6), is easier than it may appear, for several reasons.

1. United Methodists are used to singing a chorus, or refrain, after the verses of many familiar hymns and gospel songs. It has also been common for a soloist or choir to sing the verses, with the whole congregation joining in the chorus. It may be helpful for persons to think of the response as a chorus or refrain.

2. Psalm tones grew out of the experience of a culture in which the congregation did not have hymnals. They are similar to the way a small child sings and are among the earliest and easiest forms of musical expression. One does not have to read music in order to sing them; this kind of music is best learned by hearing it.

3. "Lining" (or "lining out") hymns and songs, where the people repeat each line after the leader, is an old American tradition still familiar to some congregations. This is in effect what the leader or choir is doing when introducing the response at the beginning of a psalm or canticle. It is a remarkably effective way of teaching a tune, or reminding the people of it.

4. It is not always best to sing a different psalm each Sunday. Sometimes it is more effective to sing the same psalm for several weeks or for a season of the Christian year. This is particularly true when a congregation is first learning to sing psalms.

5. It is also more effective when a congregation is first learning to sing psalms to select the way of singing the Psalter that is most appropriate to that congregation and stay with it for a period of time, rather than confuse the people by experimenting with a variety of ways in quick succession.

6. Once a congregation "catches on" to singing psalms and canticles, it is remarkably powerful and effective. This is especially true when the verses are also sung to an effective soloist or choir.

7. In many ways the key to effective psalm singing lies in the preparation and enthusiasm of the leader. If the leader has become familiar with, and enthusiastic about, a psalm or canticle, the congregation is likely to find the enthusiasm contagious.

8. More and more United Methodist singers are learning how to be effective cantors. They need not be limited to the kind of simple chanting described in No. 737. Some cantors compose or improvise their own settings of psalm verses in whatever musical style fits their own tradition or that of the congregation. Some are learning from Jewish cantorial traditions and from Black and other ethnic heritages. A congregation that is fortunate enough to have an effective cantor is likely to be especially effective in singing responses.


## C. TRADITIONAL VERSIONS OF FAMILIAR PSALMS

Several of the most familiar and beloved psalms offer both special problems and special opportunities.

Because these psalms are so familiar and beloved, new translations such as that provided in the United Methodist Liturgical Psalter may be resisted. It may be better to use these psalms in the familiar translation or to sing a familiar metrical version or paraphrase. This alternative is provided for in the hymns section of the hymnal.

*Psalm 23* is probably the most familiar and beloved of all the Psalms among United Methodists, and many have memorized it in the King James Version. For this reason, the King James Version of this psalm is found as No. 137, with the same responses as that found as No. 754 in the United Methodist Liturgical Psalter. The King James Version is also used in the Service of Death and Resurrection (No. 873). The traditional translations "valley of the shadow of death" and "I will dwell in the house of the Lord for ever" are crucial to the use of this psalm at funerals and memorial services, even though most scholars contend that the new translation is more faithful to the original Hebrew. Also included are two metrical versions of this psalm, "The King of Love My Shepherd Is" (138) and "The Lord's My Shepherd" (136), and two hymns derived from it, "He Leadeth Me" (128) and "O Thou in Whose Presence" (518).

*Psalm 24* is included in the King James Version (212) as well as in the United Methodist Liturgical Psalter (755), with the same responses for both versions. It is also paraphrased in the hymn "Lift Up Your Heads, Ye Mighty Gates" (213).

Verses from *Psalms 95 and 96* in the familiar Coverdale translation are combined in the beloved "O come, let us sing unto the Lord," which is traditionally entitled the *Venite* and which in our hymnal is entitled "Canticle of Praise to God" (91).

*Psalm 100* in the King James Version is included under the title "Canticle of Thanksgiving" (74) next to its metrical paraphrase, "All People That on Earth Do Dwell" (75).

*Psalm 130* is included in the familiar Coverdale translation under the title "Canticle of Redemption" (516), as well as in the United Methodist Liturgical Psalter (848), with the same responses for both versions. Next to it is Martin Luther's paraphrase, "Out of the Depths" (515). It is also included in the Service of Death and Resurrection (873).

## D. PSALMS WITH TROUBLING LANGUAGE

United Methodists have been protected in their earlier liturgical psalters from hearing some of the more disturbing psalm passages, but today these passages are taking on new meaning for many Christians who are learning how important it is to be honest in the presence of God. If we are not open with God about the angers and other unacceptable feelings that are in our hearts, we are not allowing God to heal us.

Psalm 137:7-9 and Psalm 139:19-22 are good examples. These were omitted in the 1966 hymnal and in the Common Lectionary but included in our new Psalter. The worship leader has the choice of announcing that they are being omitted or including them in all their harshness. In either case, the fact that the people see these words before them give the preacher opportunity to comment on why they were written and why they were included in the Bible. Offering these often-excluded angry verses can help preachers grow in their ability to preach from the whole Bible and help congregations grow in their ability to be honest about their feelings before God.

May using the United Methodist Liturgical Psalter fill you and your congregation with profound gratitude to God, whose steadfast love is from everlasting to everlasting.

# CHAPTER 8

# A SERVICE OF CHRISTIAN MARRIAGE

## A. Introduction

This Service of Christian Marriage, officially adopted by the 1984 General Conference, is one of three marriage services included in the official Ritual of The United Methodist Church, the others being "The Order for the Service of Marriage" in *The Book of Worship* (1965) of the former Methodist Church and "Holy Matrimony" in the Ritual of the former Evangelical United Brethren Church.

Which, if any, of these services of marriage should be in the hymnal? As the Hymnal Revision Committee discussed this issue, the crucial question became, What do the people in the pews need to have during the service? The hymnal, it should be remembered, is for the *people's* use. Pastors have and need additional resources, which are found in such books as *The Book of Worship*.

The two older services require only the pastor to have a copy of the text. "The Order for the Service of Marriage" in *The Book of Worship* (1965) provides for no congregational participation except in praying the Lord's Prayer and the optional singing of hymns. Since there is nothing in this service that the congregation needs to read, it was not included in *The Methodist Hymnal* of 1966 (later *The Book of Hymns*). "Holy Matrimony" in the EUB Ritual also contains nothing that the congregation needs to read and so was not included in *The Hymnal* of the EUB Church. Since these services are available to pastors in such resources as *The Book of Worship*, *The Ritual* (Methodist), *The Book of Ritual* (EUB), *Abingdon Marriage Manual*, and wedding certificates that include the text, there is still no need for the text to be in the hymnal. For this reason, *The United Methodist Hymnal* does not contain the texts of these services. It does, however, state (in No. 864) that these services are approved and indicate where they may be found.

On the other hand, the "Service of Christian Marriage" adopted by the United Methodist General Conference in 1984 provides for extensive congregational participation that can take place only if the people have the text. Leaflet sales of the text of "A Service of Christian Marriage" have been heavy. A survey showed a strong affirmative response to including the service in the hymnal. The result was a decision to include "A Service of Christian Marriage" in the hymnal.

It is clear that no one marriage service is suited for use at every wedding. "A Service of Christian Marriage," for example, is not suited to the marriage of persons who are not practicing Christians. The pastor, in consultation with each couple, can reach a responsible decision as to whether this "Service of Christian Marriage" or some other marriage service is most appropriate. The traditional orders will continue to be available. Pastors at their discretion may use marriage services adapted or created to meet the needs or wishes of a particular couple.

"A Service of Christian Marriage" is included in the hymnal for couples who wish to solemnize their marriage in a service of Christian worship with full congregational participation. Everything about the service is designed to witness that this is a *Christian* marriage. The service is parallel in structure to the Sunday service, including the proclamation of the Word together with prayer and praise. If Holy Communion is celebrated, the service is a full Service of Word and Table. Their marriage is proclaimed as a sacred covenant reflecting Christ's baptismal covenant with the Church. Both words and actions consistently reflect the belief that the husband and wife are equal partners in Christian marriage and are entering into the marriage of their own volition. Those present are understood to be an active congregation rather than simply passive observers. They give their blessing to the couple and to the marriage, they are active witnesses to the marriage, they join in the prayer and praise, and they may join together in Holy Communion.

## B. THE BIBLICAL BASIS OF CHRISTIAN MARRIAGE

The institution of marriage is based on the order of creation. "So God created man in his own image, in the image of God he created them; male and female he created them" (Gen. 1:27). In spite of the fact that most Bible translations of this passage still use the words *man, he,* and *his,* it is plain that males and females are equally created in the image of God. Jesus recalled this created equality in his teaching on divorce: "But from the beginning of creation, 'God made them male and female' " (Mark 10:6). The equality of male and female is clearly stated in such passages as Paul's declaration: "For as many of you as were baptized into Christ have put on Christ. There is neither male nor female; for you are all one in Christ Jesus" (Gal. 3:27-28).

Christian marriage is a lifelong covenant between a man and a woman who are "subject to one another out of reverence for Christ" (Eph. 5:21). It is more than a contract. "Covenant, in contrast to contract, involves giving of self unreservedly in love to the other." [10] The couple fulfill each other, and their love gives birth to new life *in* each and *through* each. Christ is the bond of unity when both their lives are centered in Christ. The couple encounters the risen Christ daily in their love for each other. They make a little family within the household of God, a "little church" in the Body of Christ.

## C. PLANNING THE SERVICE

It is the duty of the pastor "to perform the marriage ceremony after due counsel with the parties involved" (*The Book of Discipline* 1988, Par. 439.1f). An important part of this counsel is to interpret to each couple the meaning of the service in which

---

10. "Naming" in *Ritual in a New Day: An Invitation* (Nashville: Abingdon Press, 1976).

they are to be married and of the vows that they are to take in that service. If a couple choose to use the service printed in this hymnal, the pastor should take care that they understand that this is a service of *Christian* marriage. The pastor and couple should carefully go through the words and actions of the service ahead of time and consider their meaning. The pastor may wish to give the couple a copy of the booklet *Planning a Christian Wedding*, by M. Lawrence Snow (Discipleship Resources, 1988) and make use of it in the planning process.

The music that is sung or played has great power to give the service its character. Congregational singing is most desirable, and a choir may also sing. The use of vocal and instrumental music expresses the joy of the event. Note the hymns printed or listed under "Weddings" in the index (Nos. 953-954).

Because the choice of music is so important, the organist or person in charge of the music needs to be consulted in all decisions on music selection. Many congregations have adopted policies and guidelines, and musicians from outside the congregation need to be informed of them.

The organist and any other musicians involved should work together with the couple in choosing the music. Just as it is important that the integrity of the service and the musicians be respected, so also it is important that the music speak to the needs of the couple. Since congregational participation is assumed, the tastes and repertory of the people who will be present must also be considered. Difficult decisions that stretch the usual guidelines need to be made jointly so as to protect the integrity of everyone involved. Reference recordings or actually playing or singing the music can assist the couple in selecting the music that will be appropriate for their wedding.

The use of specifically Christian music is strongly encouraged. It ensures the proclamation of Christian faith and hope. Such texts and music express the joy, praise, and thanksgiving that characterize marriage in a Christian context. When choosing vocal music for services of Christian marriage, one is usually on safe ground when the text is taken from the Bible or from our official hymnal.

Holy Communion may or may not be celebrated, and it is up to the pastor and couple to decide whether it is appropriate. If it is to be celebrated, it is most important that its significance be made clear. Specifically: (1) the marriage rite is included in a service of Word and Table; (2) not only the husband and wife but the whole congregation are to be invited to receive communion, since it is our tradition to invite all Christians to the Lord's table; and (3) there should be no pressure that would embarrass those who for whatever reason choose not to receive communion.

## D. ENTRANCE

### GATHERING

The service begins when the wedding party, family, and friends assemble at the church or other appropriate location. It is most appropriate for weddings to be held in the church where the community of believers regularly gathers for worship.

*While the people gather, instrumental or vocal music may be offered.*

Since the gathering time is a part of the service, the selection of music for this part of the service, as for other parts, should follow the guidelines described above. The spirit of the music should be joy, praise, and thanksgiving.

Liturgical banners and other art forms may be displayed for the gathering or used in procession. Local church policy and customs for use of candles, flowers, and other decorations should be followed. The lighting of candles before or during the gathering, or carrying them out with the going forth, can be appropriate.

*During the entrance of the wedding party, there may be instrumental music, or a hymn, a psalm, a canticle, or an anthem.*

The climax of the gathering is the entrance of the wedding party. The man and the woman, their families, and the other members of the wedding party enter the church or place of assembly in a manner that has been previously planned and, if necessary, rehearsed. The man and the woman may enter separately or together, by themselves or with members of their families and friends. The following hymns, some of which are based on psalms, are suggested:

"All Praise to Our Redeeming Lord" (554)
"All Praise to Thee, for Thou, O King Divine" (166)
"Christ Is Made the Sure Foundation" (559)
"Come Down, O Love Divine" (475)
"Come, My Way, My Truth, My Life" (164)
"Come, Thou Almighty King" (61)
"Come, We That Love the Lord" (733)
"Jesus, Joy of Our Desiring" (644)
"Joyful, Joyful, We Adore Thee" (89)
"Let All the World in Every Corner Sing" (93)
"Love Divine, All Loves Excelling" (384)
"O God, Our Help in Ages Past" (Psalm 90) (117)
"Praise, My Soul, the King of Heaven" (Psalm 103) (66)
"Praise the Lord Who Reigns Above" (Psalm 150) (96)
"Praise to the Lord, the Almighty" (139)
"Rejoice, Ye Pure in Heart" (160, 161)
"Sing Praise to God Who Reigns Above" (126)
"The King of Love My Shepherd Is" (Psalm 23) (138)
"Ye Watchers and Ye Holy Ones" (90)
"Your Love, O God, Has Called Us Here" (647)

On the other hand, the woman and the man may enter silently and take positions visible to the assembly. The pastor(s) may join in the entrance or procession, or take a position in front of the congregation to meet the wedding party.

The way in which the couple enter can be a powerful statement in itself of the relationship of the man and the woman to each other and to their families. Entering together or moving simultaneously toward each other indicates equality. To some, for the woman to come to the man seems to suggest the subordination of the woman. What is most important is that the couple and pastor realize that there are choices and make these choices responsibly.

GREETING

The service continues with a greeting, which welcomes the people and explains the purpose of the gathering. It may be given by the pastor or by a layperson, who may be a member of the wedding party.

While the printed text of the greeting is relatively formal, the greeting may be done informally or extemporaneously and may include introductions of the participants. If the service is being conducted informally, the congregation may exchange greetings and be explicitly invited to participate. In any event, the greeting should acknowledge that those present have gathered in the name and sight of God.

Prayer may be offered before or after the greeting. If the gathering has not included a processional hymn, a hymn such as one of those mentioned above may be sung following the greeting.

## E. Declaration of Intention

### DECLARATION BY THE MAN AND THE WOMAN

The woman and man state early in the service why they are present and give their free and mutual consent to be married. Traditionally, this declaration is equivalent to the public betrothal. It should not be confused with, or a substitute for, the actual marriage vows, which come later in the service. The declaration of intention may be omitted in the public service if desired; the actual marriage vows are the essence of the service.

Christian marriage between a man and a woman is not a private matter. It presumes responsibility to both civil society and the Christian community. It is a legal contract freely entered into before witnesses. The couple announce to the congregation their intent to commit themselves unreservedly in the bond of marriage. They express without qualification or reservation their intention of lifelong fidelity and responsible family life.

### RESPONSE OF THE FAMILIES AND PEOPLE

The declaration of intention calls for a response, a blessing, by the congregation. Parents or other representatives of the families, if present, may be the first to respond.

It may be the prevailing custom or personal preference that the woman's father escort her into the service and give her hand into the hand of the man. Traditionally, giving a daughter's hand in marriage was a literal gesture consummating common law agreement about dowry and property. When the father of the bride gave her hand over to the groom, this act not only legally conveyed property but also treated the woman as a means in the process. She was property and subordinate to the man.

These specific legal connotations and obligations have become obsolete in the Service of Christian Marriage. In premarital conferences, the pastor should point out that the woman is not the property of her parents to be given away and that the parents and families of both parties may wish to respond to the declaration of intention.

The text of the service provides for such a response by the parents or other representatives of the families, if they are present. This text is adaptable to a variety of family situations that may form the context of present-day weddings. If there are children by previous marriages, they may take an active part in blessing the marriage.

The verbal blessing may be accompanied by kisses, embraces, mutual handclasps, or other gestures of affection and support. Whatever gestures are used here should apply equally to the woman and to the man.

In any case, it is most appropriate for the congregation to express its blessing and support as provided for in the service text and perhaps also by other expressions.

## PRAYER

When the congregation and couple have gathered and been greeted in God's name, and when the couple have declared their intention and been supported by the blessing of those present, it is appropriate to praise God.

## F. PROCLAMATION AND RESPONSE

### SCRIPTURE LESSON(S)

It is central in public worship that the Word of God be heard by the people. While the proclamation and response will usually be shorter in this service than in the Sunday service, it is nonetheless of central importance.

The various parts of this section may be led by the pastor(s), by members of the wedding party (including the couple), or by other family or friends.

One or more scripture lessons are read. Integral to this service is the proclamation of the good news of Jesus Christ. The man and woman should consult with the pastor(s) in selecting appropriate Scripture readings, such as the following:

Genesis 1:26-28, 31a (the creation of man and woman)
Song of Solomon 2:10-14, 16a; 8:6-7 (love strong as death)
Isaiah 43:1-7 (You are precious in God's eyes.)
Isaiah 55:10-13 (You shall go out in joy.)
Isaiah 61:10–62:3 (Rejoice in the Lord.)
Isaiah 63:7-9 (the steadfast love of the Lord)
Romans 12:1-2, 9-18 (the life of a Christian)
I Corinthians 13 (The greatest of these is love.)
II Corinthians 5:14-17 (One in Christ is a new creation.)
Ephesians 2:4-10 (God's love for us.)
Ephesians 4:1-6 (called to the one hope)
Ephesians 4:25–5:2 (members one of another)
Philippians 2:1-12 (the Christlike spirit)
Philippians 4:4-9 (Rejoice in the Lord.)
Colossians 3:12-17 (Live in love and thanksgiving.)
I John 3:18-24 (Love one another.)
I John 4:7-16 (God is love.)
Revelation 19:1, 5-9a (the wedding feast of the Lamb)
Matthew 5:1-10 (the Beatitudes)
Matthew 7:21, 24-27 (a house built upon a rock)
Matthew 22:35-40 (love, the greatest commandment)
Mark 2:18-22 (joy in Christ as at a wedding)
Mark 10:42-45 (true greatness)
John 2:1-11 (the marriage feast of Cana)
John 15:9-17 (Remain in Christ's love.)

*A hymn, psalm, canticle, anthem, or other music may be offered before or after the readings.*

Praise to God can be a bridge between the declaration of

intention and the proclamation and response—an appropriate response to the former and an introduction to the latter. It can also be an appropriate response to a scripture reading. Possible hymns, in addition to the processional hymns mentioned above, include:

"As Man and Woman" (642)
"Be Thou My Vision" (451)
"Come, Christians, Join to Sing" (158)
"O Perfect Love" (645)
"When Love Is Found" (643)
"Where Charity and Love Prevail" (549)

Psalms 23, 33, 34, 37, 67, 100, 103, 112, 145, 148, or 150, or hymns paraphrasing them, are suggested, as is Canticle of Love (No. 646). Words and music should express God's love and fidelity and the people's joy and thanksgiving. In the selection of music here, as elsewhere in the service, the organist or music director should be consulted.

## SERMON OR OTHER WITNESS TO CHRISTIAN MARRIAGE

The purpose of a wedding sermon is to proclaim to the couple and to the congregation the Christian message of God's fidelity and what it means for the wedding and the beginning of a new life together. The sermon can proclaim the promise God gives to the union and God's act in making the union possible. Such a sermon is most effective if it is brief and to the point.

The witness to Christian marriage at this point in the service may take forms other than a sermon. For example, the two charges at the beginning of the traditional service or some other appropriate classical or contemporary reading may be read, or one or more friends or family members may speak or sing.

## INTERCESSORY PRAYER

*An extemporaneous prayer may be offered, or the following may be prayed by the pastor or by all.*
The prayer printed here is an intercession for the man and the

woman and for their marriage, that their love will not only *remain* steadfast, but continue to *grow* all their days.

## G. THE MARRIAGE

### EXCHANGE OF VOWS

The marriage involves the public proclamation and acknowledgment of the couple's commitment. They marry each other in the presence of God and of the Christian community. The central moment in the marriage rite occurs when the couple promise themselves to each other for life. In this marriage covenant, the couple are the principal ministers, the pastor is an official witness of the church and of the state, and the whole congregation are not only witnesses but give their active blessing and support.

*The woman and man face each other, joining hands.*

The exchange of marriage vows by the man and the woman is their response to the gift of God's proclaimed promise, the good news of grace and love expressed in scripture. The vows printed in the text incorporate what the church understands to be the nature of the marriage covenant, which is based on the baptismal covenant. The woman and the man address each other using their Christian, or first, names.

Since this is the central act of the Service of Christian Marriage, its visual and tactile impact, as well as its verbal content, is of great importance. The couple should be clearly visible to the congregation and to the pastor(s). It should be evident that these vows are being spoken by the couple to each other and not to the pastor(s) or congregation, but it should also be evident to the congregation just what the couple are saying and doing.

The phrases "as long as you both shall live" and "until we are parted by death" do not deny the reality of a reunion after death, but mean that the surviving partner is free to remarry.

Usually the couple repeat the vows after the pastor, one line at a time. The pastor may begin by saying, "Repeat after me"; then speaking the first line, which the couple repeats; then speaking the second line, which the couple repeats; and so forth. Since the couple may speak too softly to be heard by the whole congregation, the pastor should speak the lines so that the congregation can clearly hear them. Since the couple should be looking at each other's eyes, they should not be reading the vows. Some couples memorize the vows, and the exchange of memorized vows can be very effective. On the other hand, many couples have memorized the vows, only to find that in the great emotion of the moment they still need to be prompted by the pastor.

## BLESSING AND EXCHANGE OF RINGS

The giving or exchange of rings or other tangible symbols is customary in the marriage ceremony, but it is optional. It is a visible sign of love and mutual commitment, a token and pledge of the covenant the couple has already made in their exchange of the wedding vows. It is "an outward and visible sign of an inward and spiritual grace" because the deed expresses the mutual love and trust of the couple in God and in each other. In Hispanic tradition, the husband customarily gives the wife "arras" (coins) in addition to the ring.

While the older custom was for only one ring to be given, by the husband to the wife, two rings have been exchanged in the great majority of recent weddings, signifying the equality of the marriage relationship.

*The pastor may bless the giving of rings or other symbols of the marriage.*

What the pastor blesses is not the rings in themselves, but the *giving* of rings or other symbols of the marriage. This prayer expresses the intention that these signs will be effective reminders of the couple's commitment.

The spoken pledge that accompanies the exchange confirms that the giver is making a total and absolute commitment. This pledge, like the wedding vows, is usually repeated, line by line, after the pastor. It is not specified whether the husband or wife goes first. Earlier in the service the woman makes her declaration of intention first, and the man takes his wedding vow first. The common custom is for the husband to give the wife her ring before the wife gives the husband his ring.

## DECLARATION OF MARRIAGE

*The wife and husband join hands. The pastor may place a hand on, or wrap a stole around, their joined hands.*

After the couple's commitment, the pastor announces, *not* pronounces, that they are now husband and wife. Strictly speaking, the pastor does not marry the couple, they marry each other. On the other hand, the wider community also has an important stake in the marriage, and its representation in the wedding is essential. In a Christian marriage covenant based on the Baptismal Covenant, God's action is recognized as essential. The pastor's placing a hand upon, or wrapping a stole around, the couple's joined hands symbolizes both the couple's union with each other and the supportive involvement of church, state, and community. In Hispanic tradition the witnesses (*padrinos*) will place the cord (*lazo*) over the husband and wife to symbolize their union.

Our society is increasingly aware of the significance of naming. The scriptures have much to say about the power and identity that resides in giving and invoking names. The linking of the names of the Trinity with the names of the newly married couple is a powerful Christian witness, as it also is in Baptism. Today, couples are free to choose their surnames, and whatever choice they make will both reflect and influence the character of their Christian marriage.

*A doxology or other hymn may be sung.*

The congregation may be given the opportunity to add their witness and blessing to the declaration of marriage by a simple "amen," or by singing a doxology, or an alleluia, or a hymn such as those listed under proclamation and response.

Some couples may choose to have the signing of the marriage license certificate and registry at this time in the service, perhaps during the singing of a hymn.

*Intercessions may be offered for the church and for the world.*

Since marriage takes place in the larger context of the church and the world, it is appropriate here to offer intercessions. In some situations there may be persons unable to attend the wedding whom it is appropriate to remember in prayer.

## BLESSING OF THE MARRIAGE

*The husband and wife may kneel, as the pastor prays.*

It is traditional for the husband and wife to kneel in front of the Lord's table for the blessing of the marriage, and a prie-dieu (kneeling desk) is often supplied for this purpose. Some couples, on the other hand, prefer to remain standing. The prayer recalls the link between the Baptismal Covenant and the marriage covenant and invokes God's blessing upon wife and husband and upon their marriage. The congregation indicates by their "amen" that they join with the pastor in this prayer.

## H. THANKSGIVING AND COMMUNION

*If Holy Communion is not to be celebrated, the service continues with the Lord's Prayer.*

As an expression of their communion with God and with one another, the couple and congregation pray together the most sublime Christian prayer. If the couple have knelt for the blessing of the marriage, they continue kneeling for the Lord's Prayer and then rise. The service then concludes with the Sending Forth.

Some pastors have indicated their desire to include a prayer of thanksgiving and intercession for the couple at the point in the service where the Great Thanksgiving would occur if Holy Communion were celebrated. The pastor may pray this prayer between the blessing of the marriage and the Lord's Prayer:

Most gracious God,
we give you thanks for your tender love
in making us a covenant people through our Savior
  Jesus Christ,
and for consecrating in his name
the marriage covenant of *Name* and *Name*.

Defend them from every enemy.

Lead them into all peace.

Let their love for each other be a seal upon their hearts,

a mantle about their shoulders,

and a crown upon their foreheads.

Bless them in their work and in their companionship;

in their sleeping and in their waking;

in their joys and in their sorrows;

in their life and in their death.

Finally, by your grace, bring them and all of us to
    that table

where your saints feast forever in your heavenly home;

through Jesus Christ our Lord,

who with you and the Holy Spirit lives and reigns,

one God, forever and ever. **Amen.**

*If Holy Communion is to be celebrated, the service continues with "A Service of Word and Table III"* [No. 15]

The understandings and suggestions for Holy Communion given in chapter 5 can be applied to the wedding occasion. There are, however, several matters specific to Holy Communion at weddings that should be noted.

1. The husband and wife or representatives of the congregation may bring the bread and wine to the Lord's table.

2. If the couple have been kneeling for the blessing of the marriage, they may either remain kneeling or stand for the Great Thanksgiving.

3. The pastor should make it clear to the congregation that there is an open invitation to receive communion.

4. There should be no pressure that would embarrass those who for whatever reason choose not to receive communion.

5. Although the people need no more text than is provided in "A Service of Word and Table III," the pastor will need a full Great Thanksgiving text. Such a text, designed for the marriage occasion and with the same lead-in lines and responses that the people have in front of them, is found in *The Book of Services* (pages 69-71) and also in *Holy Communion* (pages 38-39). It is:

The Lord be with you.
**And also with you.**
Lift up your hearts.
**We lift them up to the Lord.**
Let us give thanks to the Lord our God.
**It is right to give our thanks and praise.**

It is right, and a good and joyful thing,
always and everywhere to give thanks to you,
Father Almighty, Creator of heaven and earth.
You formed us in your image, male and female
    you created us.
You gave us the gift of marriage,
that we might fulfill one another.
And so with your people on earth and all the company of
heaven
we praise your name and join in their unending hymn:

**Holy, holy, holy Lord, God of power and might,**
**heaven and earth are full of your glory.**
**Hosanna in the highest.**
**Blessed is he who comes in the name of the Lord.**
**Hosanna in the highest.**

Holy are you, and blessed is your Son Jesus Christ.
By the baptism of his suffering, death, and resurrection
you gave birth to your church,
delivered us from slavery to sin and death,
and made with us a new covenant by water and the Spirit,
from which flows the covenant love of husband and wife.

On the night in which he gave himself up for us
he took bread, gave thanks to you,
broke the bread, gave it to his disciples, and said:
"Take, eat; this is my body which is given for you.
Do this in remembrance of me."
When the supper was over
he took the cup, gave thanks to you,
gave it to his disciples, and said:

"Drink from this, all of you;
this is my blood of the new covenant,
poured out for you and for many for the remission on sins.
Do this, as often as you drink it, in remembrance of me."
And so, in remembrance of these your mighty acts in Jesus
Christ,
we offer ourselves in praise and thanksgiving
as a holy and living sacrifice,
in union with Christ's offering for us,
as we proclaim the mystery of faith.

**Christ has died, Christ is risen, Christ will come again.**

Pour out your Holy Spirit on us, gathered here,
and on these gifts of bread and wine.
Make them be for us the body and blood of Christ,
that we may be for the world the body of Christ,
redeemed by his blood.
By the same Spirit bless *Name* and *Name*,
that their love for each other
may reflect the love of Christ for us
and grow from strength to strength
as they faithfully serve you in the world.
Finally, by your grace, bring them and all of us to that table
where your saints feast forever in your heavenly home.
Through your Son Jesus Christ,
with the Holy Spirit in your holy church,
all honor and glory is yours,
Almighty Father (*God*), now and forever.

**Amen.**

The Service III format leaves the pastor free to vary this Great
Thanksgiving. For example, after the line, "as they faithfully
serve you in the world," the pastor may add any or all of the
intercessions in lines 6-14 of the prayer on pages 140-41 above.
Any of the musical settings of the Great Thanksgiving (Nos.
17-25) may also be used.

## I. Sending Forth

*Here may be sung a hymn or psalm.*
See listing of hymns and psalms in the proclamation and response.

### DISMISSAL WITH BLESSING

The first two sentences are addressed primarily to the couple, and the remaining are addressed to the congregation.

### THE PEACE

*The couple and pastor(s) may greet one another, after which greetings may be exchanged through the congregation.*

This traditionally begins with the kiss and embrace of the husband and wife. Those present may also exchange the peace with one another in whatever manner is customary or appropriate. If desired, the peace may occur earlier in the service, such as before Holy Communion when it is celebrated.

### GOING FORTH

*A hymn may be sung or instrumental music played as the couple, the wedding party, and the people leave.*

As the couple, wedding party, and others leave, a hymn may be sung or instrumental music played. This music should be triumphant and joyful. Suitable recessional hymns include:

"God, Whose Love Is Reigning O'er Us" (100)
"Joyful, Joyful, We Adore Thee" (89)
"Love Divine, All Loves Excelling" (384)
"Now Thank We All Our God" (102)
"Rejoice, Ye Pure in Heart" (160, 161)

After the service has ended, the state license, church certificate, and registry should be witnessed and signed, unless this was done during the service. In marriages involving more than one church, cross-registering is desirable.

Other courtesies, such as the greeting of guests by the wedding party, can be arranged in accordance with the wishes of the couple and local church guidelines.

If a reception, wedding meal, or picnic is to be held in the church or on its adjacent grounds, a joyful procession might add to the festivities.

# CHAPTER 9

# A SERVICE OF DEATH AND RESURRECTION

## A. Introduction

This Service of Death and Resurrection, officially adopted by the 1984 General Conference, is part of a large body of resources available to the pastor in conducting funerals and memorial services.

It is included in the hymnal because it is a service of Christian worship suitable for church funerals and memorial services in which the congregation actively participates. It includes the order and text that the congregation needs. If a printed bulletin is used, it does not have to include the entire text but may simply refer the congregation to the hymnal. If there is no bulletin, hymns and scripture lessons can readily be announced.

Neither *The Methodist Hymnal* of 1966 (later *The Book of Hymns*) nor *The Hymnal* of the EUB Church (1957) included a funeral or memorial service. At that time, it was considered enough for the *pastor* to have a copy of "The Order for the Burial of the Dead" as found in *The Book of Worship* or *The Ritual* of the Methodist Church, or of "Burial of the Dead" in the EUB Ritual, or of some other collection of funeral resources. Congregational participation, if any, at funerals and memorial services was largely limited to hymns, which could be announced, and acts of worship such as the Lord's Prayer that most people could be assumed to know by heart. If more extensive congregational participation was desired, a special bulletin had to be printed.

Today an increasing number of funerals and memorial

services are services of worship with active congregational participation. To meet this need, "A Service of Death and Resurrection" has been included in the hymnal.

Pastors need more extensive resources for funerals and memorial services than the text of "A Service of Death and Resurrection" as printed in the hymnal. The full Service of Death and Resurrection as printed in *The Book of Services* contains suggested Scripture lessons, a collection of Dismissals with Blessing, a Great Thanksgiving text for use when Holy Communion is celebrated, and an Order of Committal. "The Order for the Burial of the Dead" in *The Book of Worship* and *The Ritual* (Methodist) and "Burial of the Dead" in *The Book of Ritual* (EUB) continue to be approved for use. The wide variety of settings and situations in which pastors must conduct funerals and memorial services calls for a wide choice of prayers and other acts of worship, available to pastors in such resources as the *Abingdon Funeral Manual* (revised edition, 1984).

Pastors also need to see funerals and memorial services as part of the total ministry of the church at death. The significance of these services cannot fully be understood apart from their place in the long-term ministry of the pastor and congregation to the bereaved and in the congregation's whole ongoing worship. This is thoroughly discussed on pages 115-44 of *Companion to the Book of Services*, listed in the Bibliography; and pastors are urged to read that discussion.

This service is parallel in structure to the Sunday service. It is a Service of the Word; and, if Holy Communion is included, it is a Service of Word and Table. Like the Sunday service and the Service of Christian Marriage, it is an integral part of the ongoing worship of the church.

There may be some confusion about what to call this service. It is a *funeral* when the body of the deceased is present and a *memorial service* when the body is not present. The traditional term *Burial of the Dead* is appropriate when the remains of the deceased are buried. The title "A Service of Death and Resurrection" was selected as being appropriate to any of the wide variety of situations in which this service might be used. While this service is intended primarily for use when the body of the deceased is present, it can be adapted for use at memorial services or other occasions.

## B. THE BIBLICAL BASIS OF THE SERVICE

The words "death and resurrection" in the title express clearly the twofold nature of what is done in the service: the facts of death and bereavement are honestly faced, and the gospel of resurrection is celebrated in the context of God's Baptismal Covenant with us in Christ.

The Christian gospel is a message of death and resurrection. Jesus Christ died and was raised again for our salvation. For the Christian, salvation is to die and be raised with Christ. As Romans 6:3-11 makes clear, this is acted out symbolically in baptism, daily as we "walk in newness of life," and finally in our death and resurrection. This is the theme, not only of "A Service of Death and Resurrection" but of *every* service of Christian worship. This is why this service, like the Sunday service and the Service of Christian Marriage, is based on the Baptismal Covenant.

Death is real. "Everyone must die once" (Heb. 9:27 GNV). Bereavement and grief are also real, and if the bereaved are to be comforted, they must first mourn.

But "death is swallowed up in victory." And even as we mourn we can say, "Thanks be to God, who gives us the victory through our Lord Jesus Christ" (I Cor. 15:54, 57).

## C. PLANNING THE SERVICE

It is the duty of the pastor "to counsel bereaved families and conduct appropriate funeral and memorial services" (*The Book of Discipline* 1988, Par. 439.1*h*). What is appropriate in a funeral or memorial service will vary from one situation to another, and what the pastor does should be informed by consultation with the bereaved as well as by pastoral understanding.

The pastor should be notified immediately of the death of a member or constituent of the congregation. All arrangements should be made and approved in consultation with the pastor.

These statements are in the opening rubrics of the service in the hymnal in order that churchgoers may read them and remember them when there is a death. The congregation should from time to time be reminded through other channels of communication as well.

In short, it is both common courtesy and practical wisdom that neither the pastor nor the bereaved family make plans for the service without consulting the other.

Some persons plan their own funerals while they are still alive. Pastors may wish to distribute copies of *Your Ministry of Planning a Christian Funeral*, by Thomas A. Langford, III (Discipleship Resources, 1989) and use it with persons to plan funerals.

Certain questions are obvious. Is the service in the hymnal appropriate for this particular funeral or memorial service? If so, what choices are to be made where the service provides options? Does the service need to be adapted; and if so, how? Does the situation call for a substantially different service; and if so, what kind of service?

In answering these questions the pastor should be familiar with "A Service of Death and Resurrection" and be aware of its possibilities and limitations. If called upon to conduct a funeral or memorial service for a non-Christian, for instance, the pastor would not want to say or do anything that indicated the deceased *was* a Christian and would adapt the service accordingly or use other available services or resources. If the deceased and the family are Christians in whose lives the church and its worship have been important, "A Service of Death and Resurrection" in the church would be appropriate. If "A Service of Death and Resurrection" is to be held in a funeral home rather than in church, provision should be made for providing the people with hymnals or bulletins, or else adaptations should be made to reduce congregational participation.

A good working relationship with the funeral director is important. Plans that seem simple and appropriate to the pastor may seem inappropriate or unfeasible to the funeral director, and vice versa. It is highly desirable that pastors get to know the funeral directors with whom they will be working and come to a mutual understanding and respect in their views of the funeral and its conduct.

The music that is sung or played has great power to give the service its character, Christian or otherwise. Congregational singing is most desirable, and a choir may also sing. Vocal and instrumental music is an important part of funeral and memorial services. Note the hymns printed or listed in the "Funeral and Memorial Service" (Nos. 652-656), "Death and Eternal Life" (Nos. 700-707), and "Communion of the Saints" (Nos. 708-713) sections of the hymnal, and Funeral And Memorial Services (index Nos. 941-942).

Because the choice of music is so important, the organist or person in charge of the music needs to be consulted in all decisions on music selection. Many congregations have adopted policies and guidelines, and musicians from outside the congregation need to be informed of them.

Just as it is important that the integrity of the service and of the musicians be respected, so also it is important that the wishes of the family be respected and that the tastes and abilities of the people who will be present be considered. Difficult decisions that stretch the usual guidelines need to be made jointly so as to protect the integrity of everyone involved.

Holy Communion may or may not be included in the service, and it is up to the pastor and the family to decide whether it is appropriate. As the commentary below indicates, there are several possible ways of including Holy Communion; and if it is included, planning is needed.

## D. ENTRANCE

GATHERING

*The pastor may greet the family.*

The service begins when the people begin to gather. The solemnity of the occasion will be evident, but it may be natural and supportive for pastor and friends to welcome the family and other mourners to the place of the service. Here and elsewhere in the service, the human warmth and love of the people should find natural, unforced expression.

*Music for worship may be offered while the people gather.*
*Hymns and songs of faith may be sung during the gathering.*

In the sanctuary or chapel, the people are not only gathering physically but collecting themselves spiritually as well, and the environment should be conducive to this. Before or during the gathering, candles in the chancel may be lit. Flowers and other special decorations should not obscure or dominate the cross, the Lord's table, and other Christian symbolism in the chancel. The music that is sung or played should be carefully selected for its contribution to this environment. When enough people have gathered, they may wish to sing hymns and songs of faith such as "He Leadeth Me" (128), "Precious Lord" (474), "When We Are Living" (356), or "In the Bulb There Is a Flower" (707). If a hymn is considered especially appropriate but is not familiar to the people present, having it sung by a soloist or choir would be preferable to trying to teach it at this time.

*The pall may be placed on the coffin or urn.*

There is much to be said for covering the coffin with a pall, especially when a funeral is held in the church. The same pall is used in a congregation for all funerals. This makes all coffins, however plain or extravagant, equal before the table of the Lord. A pall not only signifies the equality of all members, it also connects the service with the new life in Christ that the Christian put on at baptism, and it prefigures the purification that faith looks forward to in Christ.

Funeral palls are illustrated in the catalogs of Cokesbury and other church supply houses. They can be purchased from one of these houses or made by members of the church. Patterns or kits are available.

While funeral palls and paraments have been of various colors, the basic, or background, color of most recently made palls and paraments is white. White signifies both death and resurrection. On the one hand, white is used as a color of mourning in many African and Asian cultures. Even in Western cultures there is an association of white with death in phrases like "white as a ghost" and the use of white masks or face paint. On the other hand, white has predominantly been used in

Christian tradition and practice to symbolize resurrection, new life, joy, and celebration.

On the white background can be a cross, a crown, a sheaf of wheat, vines or branches with leaves, and other appropriate symbols. Appropriate colors for these include gold (signifying joy and celebration, green (signifying life and growth), blood red (signifying the atoning blood of Christ), and blue (signifying hope).

For each service the pall should be clean and free of wrinkles, and flowers should never be placed on top of it.

Family or friends may place the pall over the coffin. If there is to be a procession, the pall may be laid over the last pew in readiness for the arrival of the coffin and then placed on the coffin in the open sanctuary or chapel doorway just as the procession is about to begin, while the pastor speaks from the doorway so as to be heard by the people inside. If the coffin is already in place at the front of the sanctuary or chapel, the pall is placed, and the pastor speaks, in front of the people.

The words that the pastor speaks proclaim the basis of the "Service of Death and Resurrection" in the baptismal covenant. They set the human life of the deceased within the divine life of Christ that was "put on" at Baptism. At the same time, they quietly affirm in the words of I John 3:2-3 the promise of life with Christ after death. So important are these words in expressing the meaning of the service that, if a pall is *not* placed on the coffin during the gathering, these words should still be used at the funeral of a baptized Christian following the word of grace and greeting.

## THE WORD OF GRACE

*The coffin or urn may be carried into the place of worship in procession, the pastor going before it and saying the word of grace, the congregation standing. Or, if the coffin or urn is already in place, the pastor says the following in front of the congregation.*

A procession has great symbolic meaning, especially when it includes the bringing in of the coffin or urn. It acts out the coming in and the coming together of the congregation and gives physical form to the aspiration of the people toward God. A procession need not be elaborate or rigidly ordered. It may be simple, and its very simplicity can be a powerful witness. In both procession and recession, the coffin or urn should be physically carried by the pallbearers as a sign of respect, rather than being rolled in on wheels.

Arrangements should be made with the pallbearers and funeral director to bring the coffin to a position at right angles to the Lord's table. Traditionally, the head of the coffin is toward the congregation unless the deceased was ordained, in which case the head is toward the Lord's table. This suggests the position of laity sitting in the pews and clergy in the chancel. Others today prefer that all coffins be placed with the head toward the Lord's table. If Holy Communion is to be celebrated, however, the coffin may need to be located differently, so that the people can come forward to receive communion. The coffin should remain closed throughout the entire service.

During the procession, a hymn of praise may be sung, or the pastor may say the word of grace while preceding the coffin in the procession. In either case, the congregation stands during the procession.

The phrase "the word of grace" is intended to convey several meanings. "Word" means God's self-disclosure and self-giving. "Grace" suggests the active reality of God's love in calling, meeting, and dealing with the people. The printed text (John 11:25-26; Rev. 22:13; 1:18; John 14:19) is Christ-centered, just as grace is. Through sayings attributed by believers to Christ, the voice of Christ opens the service, and the mysterious presence of Christ is offered. The cosmic meaning of Christ's victory over sin and death is declared, and Christ's life is promised now and forever.

GREETING

The words used in the greeting state the purpose of the service. Our grief and our faith are both acknowledged. Naming the deceased in this moderately formal context makes the greeting personal, but not *too* personal.

*If the pall was not placed on the coffin or urn earlier, the sentences used above for that act may be used here instead.*

HYMN OR SONG

The location of the opening hymn or song in the service is at the discretion of the pastor. It may come before, during, or after the procession, after the word of grace, or after the greeting. Most appropriate here is a strong congregational hymn on the greatness and goodness of God such as "A Mighty Fortress Is Our God" (110); "For All the Saints, Who from Their Labors Rest" (711); "All Praise to Thee, for Thou, O King Divine" (166); or "God of Grace and God of Glory" (577).

PRAYER

*The following or other prayers may be offered, in unison if desired. Petition for God's help, thanksgiving for the communion of saints, confession of sin, and assurance of pardon are appropriate here.*

What constitutes appropriate prayer at this point will be indicated by the circumstances of each particular funeral. At this moment, early in the service, what are the spiritual conditions and needs of the people present? What kinds of prayer are to be offered later in the service? With an overview of the whole service and of all the elements of prayer in mind, what is the spiritual path along which the service seeks to lead the people?

People can be at very different spiritual "places" at this point in the service. They may feel an urgent need for God's help. They may feel thankful for a life well lived and want to feel a continuing communion with that life. They may feel guilt that calls for confession and pardon. Accordingly, three sample prayers are offered.

1. Prayer for God's help is placed first because it fits the situation of the bereaved and expresses the basic reality underlying all Christian prayer—our dependence upon God, and God's grace answering to our need.

2. Prayer of thanksgiving and intercession for the communion of saints is the prayer of the assembled Christian community, affirming the place of the deceased in the communion of saints and embracing those who pray on earth with those in the Church triumphant.

3. Confession and pardon are meant to deal with the sense of failure, fear, and guilt that grief often brings. At the same time, confession acknowledges sin as a kind of death from which

God's mercy can deliver us into life. The words of pardon (Rom. 8:34; I Cor. 15:57) refer again to the basic theme of death and resurrection.

Any or all of these prayers may be used, with or without the responsive call to prayer. Other prayers may be selected, or extemporaneous prayer may be offered. The local or ethnic heritage of the congregation or family will influence the choice and style of prayer. Some styles of praying are so essentially oral that they are better transmitted by hearing and remembering than by reading from the printed page. While hymnals cannot effectively include examples of such styles, they have a vital place and importance in worship.

PSALM 130

This psalm and those that follow in the proclamation and response are not used as scripture lessons but as prayer and praise. Psalm 130, whether sung or read in chorus, functions here as a Scripture song. It voices the situation of the people before God, recapitulates the drama of death and resurrection, and combines comfort and healing with salvation. It expresses judgment and mercy, fear and trust, guilt and forgiveness, the present and the future. It draws together and concludes the entrance, the first major division of the service, and serves as a bridge to the proclamation and response. Ever since John Wesley heard it sung on the day of his Aldersgate experience, Psalm 130 has been prominent in Wesleyan tradition.

The version printed in the service is taken, with modifications, from the King James Version of the Bible because of its intrinsic power and beauty. The version of Psalm 130 in the Psalter (848), or in the Canticle of Redemption (516), or in hymn 515 ("Out of the Depths I Cry to You") may be substituted.

In this service Psalm 130 also fulfills the function of the prayer for illumination in the Order of Sunday Worship. Although a separate prayer for illumination may be added if desired, the solemnity and power of Psalm 130 and the very gravity of the funeral occasion itself communicate such a sense of waiting upon God that the prayer for illumination can appropriately be omitted.

## E. PROCLAMATION AND RESPONSE

### OLD TESTAMENT LESSON

The most basic purpose of the "Service of Death and Resurrection" is to proclaim the gospel in the face of death. It is a Service of the Word. The proclamation of Scripture, therefore, is essential to this service.

The arrangement of Scripture readings follows the traditional sequence of Old Testament lesson, New Testament lesson, and Gospel. Readings should be selected to embody the integrity and fullness of the gospel and to culminate in words attributed to Jesus himself in the Gospels. This principle governs the choice of "preferred" and "recommended" readings and gives them unity, sequence, and dramatic movement. Particular situations may, of course, call for readings other than those listed here.

> *Preferred:*      Isaiah 40:1-6, 8-11, 28-31
> *Recommended:*  Exodus 14:5-14, 19-31
>                          Isaiah 43:1-3*a*, 5-7, 13, 15, 18-19, 25; 44:6, 8*a*
>                          Isaiah 55:1-3, 6-13

Isaiah 40 and its recommended alternatives strongly proclaim the Old Testament meanings of death and resurrection.

### PSALM 23

*Sung or said by the people standing.*

This is probably the Scripture passage most widely associated with funerals, and its use is generally acknowledged to be virtually essential. It is not a lesson; it is a response of prayer and praise. Preferably it should be sung—or, if necessary, spoken— by the people. Sung versions are found in the hymnal as Nos. 128, 136, 138, and 518. It may be read in unison as printed in the service. The King James Version is used, for two reasons. First, it is familiar and beloved, and many persons know it by memory, and second, it is especially suited for use at funerals and memorial services because it refers to "the valley of the shadow of death" and ends with the words "for ever," as most modern translations do not. For this reason, if Psalm 23 is read responsively at a funeral or memorial service, 137 (King James Version) will probably be preferred to 754 in the Psalter.

This psalm since ancient times has also been associated by Christians with Holy Communion. It takes on a special meaning when the "Service of Death and Resurrection" includes communion.

## NEW TESTAMENT LESSON

*Preferred:*    I Corinthians 15:1-8, 12-20, 35-44, 53-55, 57-58
                Revelation 21:1-7, 22-27; 22:1-5
*Recommended:* Romans 8:1-2, 5-6, 10-11, 14-19, 22-28, 31-32, 35-39
                II Corinthians 4:5-18
                Ephesians 1:15-23; 2:1, 4-10
                I Peter 1:3-9, 13, 21-25
                Revelation 7:2-3, 9-17

First Corinthians 15 forthrightly proclaims the theme of death and resurrection with reason and passion. Death and resurrection are declared as historical event and then interpreted. This epistle is appropriately followed by the soaring passages of Revelation 21 and 22.

## PSALM OR HYMN

*Recommended, either here or after the Old Testament Lesson:*
Psalms 42 (No. 777), 43 (No. 778), 46 (Nos. 780, 110, or 534), 90 (Nos. 809 or 117), 91 (Nos. 810 or 502), 103 (Nos. 824, 66, or 139), 116 (No. 837), 121 (No. 844), 139 (No. 854), 145 (No. 857), or 146 (Nos. 858 or 60).

A psalm or hymn following the New Testament lesson, like Psalm 23 after the Old Testament lesson, follows the rhythm of call and response that is so basic to worship. Perhaps more in funerals and memorial services than at other times, pastors are tempted to read an unbroken succession of scripture passages until the people's attention lags. It is much more effective for the people to sing, or read responsively, at this point.

So many psalms in addition to Psalm 23 are appropriate at funerals that serious consideration should be given to singing, or responsively speaking, one of the above psalms or a hymn paraphrase.

Of course, some other hymn or song may be found appropriate to the occasion. While people's feelings and fond associations are important and need to be taken into consideration, it is generally preferable that music at this point be sung by the people, be organic to the movement of the service, and be theologically consistent with the gospel of death and resurrection. At the same time, all music is evocative, and the meanings it suggests may proclaim the gospel more effectively than the rational content of the words would lead one to expect.

## GOSPEL LESSON

*Preferred:*　　John 14:1-10a, 15-21, 25-27
*Recommended:*　Luke 24:13-35; John 11:1-5, 20-27, 32-35, 38-44

The readings culminate in the great assurance of John 14 and its recommended alternatives.

## SERMON

*A sermon may be preached, proclaiming the gospel in the face of death. It may lead into, or include, the following acts of naming and witness.*
The sermon, however brief, should be a proclamation of the gospel of Jesus Christ in the face, not only of death in general, but also of the particular grief of this occasion. While the sermon should not be primarily a eulogy, it should not be so depersonalized that reference to the deceased and the mourners is eliminated.

The optional acts of *naming* and *witness* may help make the proclamation all that it should be. These may follow the sermon as separate acts, or be included in the sermon.

## NAMING

*The life and death of the deceased may be gathered up by the reading of a memorial or appropriate statement, or in other ways, by the pastor or others.*

The act of naming is intended to make the service more personal by singling out and lifting up the individual, human selfhood of the deceased, and by identifying, implicitly or explicitly, the relationships of the deceased to the mourners. This may be done by the reading of an obituary or memorial statement, or in other ways. It may be done by the pastor, or by others. The act can recognize particular achievements. It can be a means of summarily reviewing and cherishing the life of the deceased, and then of letting go. For a Christian, it declares again the name connected with baptism, when the deceased was symbolically buried and raised with Christ and grafted as a member of Christ's Body, the Church.

Naming of the deceased can also be effectively done at other times—elsewhere in this service, at congregational worship on the Sunday following the death or funeral, on All Saints Day or Sunday, and on a wide variety of memorial and commemorative occasions.

## WITNESS

*Family, friends, and members of the congregation may briefly voice their thankfulness to God for the grace they have received in the life of the deceased and their Christian faith and joy. Signs of faith, hope, and love may be exchanged.*

Acts of witness are intended to direct thought to the deceased, but within the context of God's grace.

One form of witness is a brief *eulogy—words* of tribute or appreciation. This is appropriate, but the full meaning of the word *witness* warns against *untruthful* eulogy. Whatever was good in the life and accomplishments of the deceased should be acknowledged as gifts of God's grace, and it is God above all who deserves thanks and praise. It is good to explain this in advance to those who are invited to offer witness.

Another form of witness is the reading of selected messages and tributes from mourners unable to be present.

Still another form of witness is a brief reading from a favorite book or poem. Such readings are common in funerals and memorial services, and they can be appropriate acts of witness in "A Service of Death and Resurrection." They should *not*, however, take the place of Scripture or express a message that undercuts the gospel of death and resurrection.

There are other forms of witness—signs of faith, hope, and love. These are particularly helpful when persons have difficulty putting their witness into words, and they are not limited to this one time in the service. (1) The Peace—handclasp or embrace, with or without words. (2) The bringing in or placing of flowers, perhaps of the kind most loved by the deceased. (3) The bringing in or placing of a sheaf of wheat, expressing the symbolism of John 12:24 and I Corinthians 15:37. (4) The display of favorite pictures. (5) Symbols of the vocation or accomplishment of the deceased—a tool, a garment, an award, a product of the deceased's work. (6) Recognition of people who have come to the service from a considerable distance, since their travel is in itself a witness. Faith and imagination may suggest other signs.

The pastor may incorporate in the announcement at this time of witness the words of Paul:

> Praise be to the God and Father of our Lord Jesus Christ, the all-merciful Father, the God whose consolation never fails us! He comforts us in all our troubles, so that we in turn may be able to comfort others in any trouble of theirs and to share with them the consolation we ourselves receive from God (II Cor. 1:3-4 NEB).

In some situations, it may be better to separate this time of witness from the service itself and incorporate it into an informal time of sharing before or after the service.

## HYMN OR SONG

In the rhythm of call and response that is so basic to our worship, the *proclamation* of the gospel of death and resurrection calls for *response* from the people. Two congregational responses are here suggested. In them, the people offer their trust in God's saving action in Jesus Christ as the event on which they take their stand and by which they are prepared to live and die.

A congregational hymn or song of faith is an appropriate response to the gospel message that has been heard. Many persons and congregations express their faith and trust more fully by singing than by speaking.

## CREED

*If the creed has not been preceded by, it may be followed by, a hymn or musical response.*

The second suggested congregational response is the creed. While any of the affirmations of faith (Nos. 880-889) may be used, the Apostles' Creed (No. 881 or 882) is recommended because of its special set of meanings at "A Service of Death and Resurrection." By echoing the profession of faith made at our baptism, it recalls the fact of our baptism and the reality of our baptismal covenant and faith. It singles out and avows the death and resurrection of Jesus Christ as decisive for our destiny. As response to proclamation, it is a reoffering of ourselves to God.

These responses are optional. This service may be used on occasions when such a corporate expression of Christian faith by those present would be impossible, or lack integrity. Where a witness to the gospel has been made, but where only a fraction of those present could honestly respond in faith, it may be best to omit the response or to have a musical response of faith offered by a soloist or a small ensemble.

A note of caution, however, is in order. Because funerals and memorial services so commonly include persons other than committed Christians, it is easy to rationalize a pattern of omitting congregational acts of faith. It is important to remember all the persons present who want and need the opportunity to express their faith and to remember that those present who cannot with integrity do so can quietly refrain from singing or speaking.

# F. COMMENDATION

## PRAYERS

*One or more of the following prayers may be offered, or other prayers may be used. They may take the form of a pastoral prayer, a series of shorter prayers, or a litany. Intercession, commendation of life, and thanksgiving are appropriate here.*

All that has gone before in this service leads up in a natural movement and momentum to the act of *commendation*. This is the primary and most essential response to the proclamation of the gospel that has taken place earlier in the service. This time might also be called "the offering of life." It takes the form of prayer, in which we offer, or commend, the life of the deceased and our own lives to God. Its supreme model is Jesus' prayer on the cross: "Father, into thy hands I commend my spirit" (Luke 23:46 KJV).

If the service of committal normally held at the grave or the place of cremation is to be included in this service instead, it may be shortened and substituted for the commendation. Since, however, the committal should whenever possible be conducted at the burial site and often cannot be held immediately following the funeral, and because many who attend the funeral may not attend the committal, a committal *outside of* this service is no substitute for the commendation *within* this service.

Three prayers are printed in the text. The first emphasizes our commendation of one another to God in prayer. The second combines commendation of the deceased to God with commendation of ourselves to God. The third is purely a commendation of the deceased to God. Other prayers may be used.

Many pastors in the commendation lay hands on the coffin to add the dimension of "body language" to the prayer.

These prayers may need to be adapted, or other prayers substituted, if the deceased was not a Christian. On the other hand, these prayers may be more appropriate than they might at first appear. Pastoral sensitivity is of crucial importance here.

## G. IF HOLY COMMUNION IS NOT CELEBRATED

### PRAYER OF THANKSGIVING

This is a prayer of thanks and praise for God's love in creation and redemption as the reality on which faith takes its ultimate stand. Praise and thanksgiving for this love is the first and last word in Christian prayer; it frames everything else, even suffering and sorrow.

### THE LORD'S PRAYER (Nos. 894-896)

This most sublime of prayers is the natural climax toward which the prayer of thanksgiving moves. It gathers up all other prayers and is probably the most universal bond of Christian faith. Its final ascription of power and glory, ending with the word *forever*, seals everything else with a doxology of invincible faith and joy.

### HYMN

This should, if possible, be sung by the congregation. The doxology "Praise God, from Whom All Blessings Flow" (No. 95) is one possibility and is well enough known that many will sing it from memory. See the list of suggested opening hymns on page 153 for other hymns that might be appropriate at this time.

If this is a recessional hymn, it follows, rather than precedes, the dismissal with blessing. The recession may form and proceed in approximately the same order as the procession.

### DISMISSAL WITH BLESSING

The term *dismissal* means "sending forth" and rightly incorporates into the "Service of Death and Resurrection" the congregation's missional nature. The death and resurrection theme of the service is the same theme the Christian is to live out in the world. While it may seem odd to send people forth in mission at the very time when as mourners they are likely to feel most weak, passive, and "in shock," the fact is that those very people are at that very moment being sent forth on a very demanding part of their Christian mission—namely, continuing in the days and weeks ahead to uphold and to minister to one another in their common grief and mourning. To be strengthened for these tasks, they surely need God's *blessing*. This dismissal with blessing should be spoken by the pastor face-to-face with the standing congregation, not from the rear of the church or funeral home.

The following scriptural and traditional dismissals with blessing are included in *The Book of Services* for the pastor's use. They do not need to be read by the people and are, therefore, not printed in the hymnal. The pastor may use one or more of these, or some other dismissal with blessing.

Now may the God of peace
who brought again from the dead our Lord Jesus,
the great shepherd of the sheep,
by the blood of the eternal covenant,
equip you with everything good that you may do his will,
working in you that which is pleasing in his sight,
through Jesus Christ, to whom be glory for ever and ever.
**Amen.**                              (Heb. 13:20-21)

The peace of God which passes all understanding
keep your hearts and minds
in the knowledge and love of God,
and of his Son Jesus Christ our Lord.
And the blessing of God Almighty,
the Father, Son, and Holy Spirit,
be among you and remain with you always.
**Amen.**

Now may the Father
from whom every family in heaven and earth is named,
according to the riches of his glory,
grant you to be strengthened with might
through his Spirit in your inner being,
that Christ may dwell in your hearts through faith;
that you, being rooted and grounded in love,
may be able to comprehend with all the saints

what is the breath and length and height and depth,
and to know the love of Christ which surpasses knowledge,
that you may be filled with all the fullness of God.
**Amen.**                                   (Eph. 3:14-19 paraphrase)

Now to the [One] who by the power at work within us
is able to do far more abundantly than all that we ask or think,
to [this God] be glory in the Church and in Christ Jesus
to all generations, for ever and ever.
**Amen.**                                              (Eph. 3:20-21)

If there is no recession, the pastor may take up a position before the coffin and precede it as it is borne from the place of the service to the hearse, again carried by pallbearers. The pastor should consult with the funeral director before the funeral about procedures at this point.

There may be music during the departure of the people, but there is much to be said for not having music here and instead concluding the service in silence.

*A service of committal follows at the final resting place.*

The committal is central to the "Service of Death and Resurrection," and the text of the committal was adopted by the 1984 General Conference as part of the service. This text does not appear in the hymnal because the people normally will not have hymnals at the committal. The pastor, however, needs to have the committal text, which is found in *The Book of Services* (pages 87-91) and also below.

## H. If Holy Communion Is Celebrated

*The pastor may administer Holy Communion to all present who wish to share at the Lord's table, using "A Service of Word and Table III."*

Holy Communion at funerals and memorial services is unfamiliar to many people, but this ancient Christian practice has begun to be recovered by United Methodists who understand how ancient and appropriate it is at the death of a Christian.

This practice, which goes back at least to the third century and perhaps to the Church's beginnings, probably arose from the natural wish of the living to maintain union with departed relatives and friends. Holy Communion is the deepest expression of "the communion of saints," our union in Christ with all those of "all times and in all places" who constitute the Body of Christ. In it we join not only with Christians around the world but also "with all the company of heaven" in praise and thanksgiving. This dimension of Holy Communion was precious to John and Charles Wesley. A study of the hymns listed under "Communion of the Saints" in the hymnal will show how beautifully Christian devotion has reflected on this theme.

All this is closely related to the fact that Holy Communion acts out and celebrates the gospel of death and resurrection. In it, the facets of sorrow and joy, penitence and faith, brokenness and healing, all are expressed as parts of a unified whole. It is not only the supper instituted the night before Jesus died, it is the risen Christ recognized "in the breaking of the bread," and it is a foretaste of the heavenly banquet and of our reunion with those we have loved on earth.

Appropriate as Holy Communion is at some funerals and memorial services, there are other situations where it is not appropriate. It should not be celebrated at a funeral or memorial service for the unchurched or the non-Christian. It is much more naturally and appropriately celebrated at a church funeral or memorial service than in a funeral home. It should not be celebrated where it is not desired or understood as appropriate, or where it is likely to cause controversy. Education will be needed if this practice is to be successfully introduced to congregations where it has been unknown. Only after consultation with the family of the deceased, or with the deceased before death, should it be celebrated.

The understandings and suggestions for Holy Communion given in chapter 5 can be applied to funeral and memorial occasions. There are, however, several matters that need special mention.

1. Family members and friends of the deceased may bring the

bread and wine to the Lord's table either in an opening procession or as the people are about to turn to Service III for Holy Communion. They may later assist in the distribution of communion.

2. The pastor should make it clear to the congregation that there is an open invitation to receive communion.

3. There should be no pressure that would embarrass those who for whatever reason choose not to receive communion.

4. It is appropriate that there be a doxology or other hymn of praise and thanksgiving after the communion.

5. The discussion of the closing hymn, dismissal with blessing, and committal on pages 162-64 above applies equally when Holy Communion is celebrated.

6. Alternatively, Holy Communion may be celebrated before a common meal following the service or with the family at some time following the service. In such a case, it may be regarded as a continuation of the service, and nothing need be repeated. The pastor presides.

7. Although the people need no more text than is provided in "A Service of Word and Table III," the pastor will need a full Great Thanksgiving text. Such a text, designed for "A Service of Death and Resurrection" and with the same lead-in lines and responses that the people have in front of them, is found in *The Book of Services* (pages 85-87) and also in *Holy Communion* (pages 40-41), where it is printed in a format suited for convenient use at the service itself. It is as follows:

The Lord be with you.
**And also with you.**
Lift up your hearts.
**We lift them up to the Lord.**
Let us give thanks to the Lord our God.
**It is right to give our thanks and praise.**

It is right,
that we should always and everywhere give thanks to you,
Father Almighty, Creator of heaven and earth,
through Jesus Christ our Lord,

who rose victorious from the dead
and comforts us with the blessed hope of everlasting life.
And so, with your people on earth and all the company of heaven,
we praise your name and join their unending hymn:

**Holy, holy, holy Lord, God of power and might,**
**heaven and earth are full of your glory.**
**Hosanna in the highest.**
**Blessed is he who comes in the name of the Lord.**
**Hosanna in the highest.**

Holy are you, and blessed is your Son Jesus Christ.
By the baptism of his suffering, death, and resurrection
you gave birth to your church,
delivered us from slavery to sin and death,
and made with us a new covenant by water and the Spirit.
When the Lord Jesus ascended
he promised to be with us always
in the power of your Word and Holy Spirit.

On the night in which he gave himself up for us
he took bread, gave thanks to you,
broke the bread, gave it to his disciples, and said:
"Take, eat; this is my body which is given for you.
Do this in remembrance of me."
When the supper was over
he took the cup, gave thanks to you,
gave it to his disciples, and said:
"Drink from this, all of you;
this is my blood of the new covenant,
poured out for you and for many for the forgiveness of sins.
Do this, as often as you drink it,
in remembrance of me."

And so, in remembrance of these your mighty acts in Jesus Christ,
we offer ourselves in praise and thanksgiving
as a holy and living sacrifice,
in union with Christ's offering for us,
as we proclaim the mystery of faith.

**Christ has died, Christ is risen, Christ will come again.**

Pour out your Holy Spirit on us, gathered here,
and on these gifts of bread and wine.
Make them be for us the body and blood of Christ,
that we may be for the world the body of Christ,
redeemed by his blood.
By your Spirit make us one with Christ,
one with each other,
and one in communion with all your saints,
especially *Name*
and all those most dear to us.
Finally, by your grace, bring them and all of us to that table
where your saints feast forever in your heavenly home.
Through your Son Jesus Christ,
with the Holy Spirit in your holy church,
all honor and glory is yours,
Almighty Father (*God*), now and for ever.

**Amen.**

The Service III format leaves the pastor free to vary this Great Thanksgiving as may be appropriate to the occasion. For example, parts of the prayer of thanksgiving printed in the text for use when Holy Communion is not celebrated may be included in the Great Thanksgiving—lines 1-9 after the line, "and comforts us with the blessed hope of everlasting life," and lines 11-13 after the line, "Holy are you, and blessed is your Son Jesus Christ." Any of the musical settings of the Great Thanksgiving (Nos. 17-25) may also be used.

# I. A SERVICE OF COMMITTAL[11]

*This order is intended primarily for burial in the ground. However, it can be adapted for cremation or the interment of ashes, for burial above*

---

11. From *The Book of Services*, pages 87 ff. Copyright © 1985 by The United Methodist Publishing House. Used by permission.

*ground or at sea, or when the body is donated for medical purposes.*
*The pastor should preside.*
*Prayers and lections appropriate for a service for a child or youth, or for*
*other distinctive occasions, may be used instead of the following. When*
*the people have gathered, one or more of the following are said:*

In the midst of life we are in death; from whom can we seek
  help?
Our help is in the name of the Lord, who made heaven and
  earth.
He who raised Jesus Christ from the dead
will give life to your mortal bodies also
through his Spirit which dwells in you.

Behold, I tell you a mystery!
We shall not all die, but we shall all be changed.
This perishable nature must put on the imperishable,
this mortal the immortal.
Then shall come to pass the saying, "Death is swallowed up in
  victory."
"O death, where is your sting? O grave, where is your victory?"
Thanks be to God who gives us the victory
through our Lord Jesus Christ.

Therefore my heart is glad and my spirit rejoices.
My body also shall rest in hope.
You, Lord, will show me the path of life.
In your presence is fullness of joy.
At your right hand are pleasures forever more.

*The following prayer is offered:*

Let us pray.
O God, you have ordered this wonderful world
and know all things in earth and in heaven.
Give us such faith that by day and by night,
at all times and in all places,
we may without fear commit ourselves and those dear to us
to your never-failing love,
in this life and in the life to come.
**Amen.**

*One of the following or other scriptures may be read.*

Blessed be the God and Father of our Lord Jesus Christ! By his great mercy we have been born anew to a living hope through the resurrection of Jesus Christ from the dead, and to an inheritance which is imperishable, undefiled, and unfading, kept in heaven for you. In this you rejoice, though now for a little while you suffer trials so that the genuineness of your faith may prove itself worthy at the revelation of Jesus Christ. Without having seen him, yet you love him; though you do not now see him, you believe in him and rejoice with unutterable and exalted joy. As the harvest of your faith you reap the salvation of your souls (I Pet. 1:3-4, 6-7*a*, 7*c*-9 RSV altered).

Jesus said: "Truly, truly I say to you, unless a grain of wheat falls into the earth and dies, it remains alone; but if it dies, it bears much fruit. He who loves his life loses it, and he who hates his life in this world will keep it for eternal life. If any one serves me, he must follow me; and where I am, there shall my servant be also; if any one serves me, the Father will honor him" (John 12:24-26).

*Standing at the head of the coffin and facing it, while earth is cast upon it as the coffin is lowered into the grave, the pastor says the following:*

Almighty God, into your hands we commend your child *Name*, in sure and certain hope of resurrection to eternal life through Jesus Christ our Lord. **Amen.**

This body we commit to the ground
(*or* the elements, *or* its resting place),
earth to earth, ashes to ashes, dust to dust.
Blessed are the dead who die in the Lord.
Yes, says the Spirit,
they rest from their labors and their works do follow them.

*One or more of the following or other prayers is offered.*

Let us pray.
Gracious God,
we thank you for those we love but see no more.

Receive into your arms your servant *Name*,
and grant that increasing in knowledge and love of you,
*he/she* may go from strength to strength
in service to your heavenly kingdom;
through Jesus Christ our Lord.
**Amen.**

Almighty God,
look with pity upon the sorrow of your servants,
for whom we pray.
Amidst things they cannot understand,
help them to trust in your care.
Bless them and keep them.
Make your face to shine upon them and be gracious to them.
Lift up your countenance upon them and give them peace.
**Amen.**

O God, whose days are without end,
make us deeply aware of the shortness and uncertainty
of our human life.
Raise us from sin into love and goodness,
that when we depart this life we may rest in Christ
and receive the blessing he has promised
to those who love and serve him:
"Come, you blessed of my Father,
receive the kingdom prepared for you
from the foundation of the world."
Grant this, merciful Father,
through Jesus Christ our Mediator and Redeemer.
**Amen.**

O Lord, support us all the day long of our troubled life,
until the shadows lengthen and the evening comes,
and the busy world is hushed,
and the fever of life is over and our work is done.
Then in your mercy grant us a safe lodging,
and a holy rest, and peace at the last;
through Jesus Christ our Lord.
**Amen.**

(Commonly attributed to John Henry Newman, 1801–1890)

Eternal God, you have shared with us the life of *Name*.
Before *he/she* was ours, *he/she* is yours.
For all that *Name* has given us to make us what we are,
for that of *him/her* which lives and grows in each of us,
and for *his/her* life that in your love will never end,
we give you thanks.
As now we offer *Name* back into your arms,
comfort us in our loneliness,
strengthen us in our weakness,
and give us courage to face the future unafraid.
Draw those of us who remain in this life closer to one another,
make us faithful to serve one another,
and give us to know that peace and joy which is eternal life;
through Jesus Christ our Lord.
**Amen.**

*The Lord's Prayer may follow.*
*A hymn or song may be sung.*
*The pastor dismisses the people with the following or another blessing:*
Now unto him who is able to keep you from falling,
and to present you faultless
before the presence of his glory
with exceeding joy,
to the only God our Savior
be glory and majesty, dominion and power,
through Jesus Christ our Lord,
both now and forever more.
**Amen.**


# J. COMMENTARY ON THE COMMITTAL

Pastoral judgment will determine how long the committal service should be and what it should include. Committal services are often too brief, when an interval has elapsed between funeral and committal and when numbers of people attend the committal who were not present at the funeral. Options in this committal service enable it to be expanded. If it is necessary to include the committal as part of the funeral service, the order should be shortened as provided for and substituted for the commendation, as was discussed above.

Clearly, the poignancy of this moment calls for great sensitivity, both liturgically and pastorally. The very variety of occasions of committal—burial in the ground of the body or its ashes, entombment above ground, burial at sea, donation of the body for medical purposes, and scattering of ashes—underscores this need. This order is intended primarily for burial in the ground. It can be adapted, however, for cremation and the interment or scattering of ashes, for burial above ground or at sea, or when the body is donated for medical purposes.

Because of the significance of ceremony and symbol, the pastor should come to a clear understanding in advance with the funeral director concerning all parts of the ceremony.

## GATHERING

In most situations, the people will gather informally at the grave. Since the surrounding space, weather, numbers in attendance, and custom affect the physical movement of the people, the manner of gathering and the arrangement of the assembly needs to be worked out with care and adaptability. Possibly an informal procession of all the people—led by the pastor, followed by the pallbearers carrying the coffin and then by the family—may voice Christian meaning better than detaining the people until the coffin is in place.

Too smooth or self-conscious or furtive attempts to lessen the starkness of the occasion, while usually well meant, are false. The very earthiness, even unexpected awkwardness, of physical movement in procession and in carrying and placing the coffin can contribute honesty and reality to the moment. The people, likewise, need not be herded into rows; an informal circle around the grave, for example, may better express Christian meaning. The pastor should stand at the head of the grave and of the unlowered coffin.

## OPENING SENTENCES

One or more of the opening sentences in the text may be spoken. They embody a sequence of devotion that voices the gospel of death and resurrection. They include a portion of a ninth-century antiphon used in the Episcopal *Book of Common Prayer*, Psalm 124:8, Romans 8:11, parts of I Corinthians 15:51-57, and Psalm 16:9, 11. They should be spoken to the people loudly enough to be heard.

## OPENING PRAYER

This prayer is revised from traditional sources and links the acts of committal of the deceased with the self-offering of the people.

## SCRIPTURE

The scripture readings (I Pet. 1:3-4, 6-7a, 7c-9; John 12:24-26) proclaim the gospel of death and resurrection. Other scripture appropriate to the occasion may be substituted.

## THE COMMITTAL

The committal is action accompanied by words. The pastor at this moment faces the coffin—not necessarily the people— turning, if need be, to do so.

The committal sentences open with Jesus' prayer of committal from the cross, name the deceased by Christian (first) name, and include elements from the Church's traditional liturgies. The concluding sentences are from Revelation 14:13.

As indicated, alternative words are to be used when the body is not in fact being committed to "the ground." The words *the elements* are appropriate at cremation, and the words *its resting place* are appropriate when that resting place is not in the ground.

It is desirable that the coffin be lowered at this point in the service, if possible beginning with the words, "This body we commit to the ground." Less preferably, the coffin may be lowered immediately after the final blessing. It greatly detracts from the integrity and symbolic power of the service to wait and lower the coffin after the mourners have left.

If possible, real earth from the grave—not flowers, or sand

from envelopes—should be cast on the coffin. This should be done by the pastor, not the funeral director. Simultaneously, earth may be cast on the coffin by family members or by other mourners if desired. Earth or flowers may be dropped onto the lowered coffin after the final blessing as a symbol of respect, committal, and farewell by other mourners if desired. Arrangements for these symbolic actions should be planned in advance with the funeral director and family, although spontaneous expressions should not be ruled out.

## CLOSING PRAYERS

The choice of prayers at the close of the committal depends on the needs of the people, on the desired length of the service, on whether the committal service is held separately from the funeral service or included in it, and on the pastor's liturgical instinct and sensitivity. Other prayers than those printed may, of course, be used. Prayers from the concluding section of "A Service of Death and Resurrection" may also be used. Extemporary prayer by the pastor may also be appropriate.

The first four prayers in the text are adapted from traditional liturgies of the Church. This sequence of four prayers constitutes a unity that includes thanksgiving, intercession, and petition for God's grace.

The last prayer is contemporary and combines in itself these elements of thanksgiving, intercession, and petition.

Places in the prayers where the first name of the deceased is spoken or where masculine or feminine pronouns need to be inserted should be noted.

The Lord's Prayer may follow.

## HYMN OR SONG

A hymn or song may be sung at this point if the service will not be unduly prolonged and if music here is not emotionally overwhelming. Although the people will not have hymnals, sometimes one or two stanzas of a familiar hymn, or a familiar doxology or chorus, can be sung from memory.

## DISMISSAL WITH BLESSING

This blessing (Jude 24-25), given by the pastor facing the people, stresses the character of God as able to guard the Christian amid frailty and vicissitude until the day of Christ's coming in final victory. As ascription and doxology, it also offers the entire service as an act of worship to God. The text is taken mainly from the King James Version because of its poetic quality.

## GOING FORTH

After the dismissal with blessing the people and funeral director usually look to the pastor for some physical gesture or movement that signals the going forth. The pastor may approach the bereaved family or other mourners in quiet farewell or accompany them as they leave.

On occasion, however, if the emotional intensity is not too great and if weather and other circumstances permit, pastor and people may wish to tarry and to greet and visit with one another in a natural way.

CHAPTER 10

# ORDERS OF DAILY PRAISE AND PRAYER

## A. Introduction

From the earliest days of the Church, Christian worshipers saw the rising of the sun and the lighting of the evening lamps as symbolic of Christ's victory over death. *The United Methodist Hymnal* now contains two "Orders of Daily Praise and Prayer"—"An Order for Morning Praise and Prayer" and "An Order for Evening Praise and Prayer"—that are designed to help United Methodists celebrate daily the life, death, and resurrection of Jesus Christ.

Prayer and praise services have always been an important part of corporate worship in The United Methodist Church and in its predecessor denominations. United Methodists today regularly pray together in family prayer time; in midweek prayer meetings and prayer groups; in Sunday school; in United Methodist Women, United Methodist Men, and United Methodist Youth Fellowship meetings; in the Emmaus and Chrysalis movements; in Covenant Discipleship groups; in the Order of Saint Luke and the Disciplined Order of Christ; in services of healing; and in many other settings. Significant resources have facilitated this corporate prayer. Particularly noteworthy are the many publications of The Upper Room, such as *The Upper Room* daily devotional guide, *The Upper Room Disciplines, alive now! A Guide to Prayer, The Upper Room Worship Book*, and *A Daily Lectionary*. Prayer together is alive and well among United Methodists.

The orders in the hymnal are sensitive to corporate prayer as

177

now observed by United Methodists, yet offer a distinctive new direction for corporate prayer. A brief history of daily corporate prayer will put these orders in context.

## B. BIBLICAL AND HISTORICAL BACKGROUND

Corporate prayer in the Christian Church has a rich and complex history. In all ages and places, Christians have gathered to sing praises and offer prayers to God. From simple patterns in the formative years of the Church, such prayers have evolved into a multitude of services.

Judaism in the time of Jesus encouraged daily prayer. At the heart of prayer was the Shema (Deut. 6:4-9). The children of Abraham and Sarah said this prayer as they rose and lay down and taught it to their children. Corporately, Jews followed a threefold pattern of prayer: in the morning, afternoon, and evening (Ps. 55:17; Dan. 6:10). Governed by the rhythm of the sun, they both remembered God's mighty acts and invoked God's active presence in the community. Such prayer services resembled temple worship, yet without cultic sacrifices. Following such prayer—at least on Saturday, Monday, and Wednesday—a second service followed, what we would call a "Service of the Word." During a "Service of the Word," the Torah (the first five books of the Bible) was read in sequence and, in a later development, interspersed with psalms. Following the destruction of the Temple in the year 70, the services of prayer and services of the Word were institutionalized in synagogue worship.

The New Testament records new developments in corporate prayer. Jesus participated both in Sabbath worship and in daily prayer governed by the sun (Mark 1:35; Matt. 14:23). Observing times of intense personal prayer himself, Jesus also encouraged his disciples to pray together daily. To aid their prayer, Jesus taught his followers his own unique prayer: the Lord's Prayer (Matt. 6:7-13; Luke 11:2-4). Following the example of Jesus, first-century Christians created a pattern of prayer that both borrowed from Jewish prayer forms and added to them unique understandings of how God was manifest in Jesus Christ. Prayer continued to be observed daily in the morning, afternoon, and evening. Guided by leaders of the community, Christians gathered in synagogues, the Temple, and in homes for prayer.

Distinctively Christian features evolved as such corporate prayer became Christ-centered. The Lord's Prayer replaced the Shema. Christological hymns such as Philippians 2:5-11 replaced some of the psalms. The whole Psalter was interpreted in the light of Christ. God was called "Abba." Jesus was referred to as "Lord." Often, after a time of prayer, a Service of Word and Table followed (Acts 20:7-12).

The pattern of first-century Christian prayer was simple: praise and proclamation of the mystery of the life, death, and resurrection of Christ were followed by petition and intercession (Phil. 4:6; Col. 4:2; I Thess. 5:16-18). The services were not long and didactic, because they were not intended to read and teach the Scriptures. Rather, they were short and exclamatory, offering thanksgiving for Jesus Christ and praying for God's love. In an oppressive culture and for these persecuted communities, such simple, brief, and focused rites enabled the struggling community to survive.

The church in the second and third centuries began to establish set patterns of daily prayer. Early church leaders such as Clement, Origen, Tertullian, Cyprian, and especially Hippolytus suggested more formal patterns of prayer. In the morning, the basic pattern included a psalm, a bidding prayer, a Christianized Shema or the Lord's Prayer, and dismissal. Prayer also was encouraged in the third and ninth hours to correspond to the hours of Christ's passion. In the evening, prayer included a lighting of the lamps with Psalm 141, a Christianized Shema or the Lord's Prayer, thanksgiving, blessing, and dismissal. This service would often be followed by a "Service of the Word" that included the reading of Scripture and teaching or preaching.

By the fourth century, a major division developed in the services of daily prayer between the cathedral (or congregational) pattern of prayer and the monastic pattern of prayer. This division had significant impact on the church and still affects prayer today. The unique characteristic of these United Methodist "Orders of Daily Praise and Prayer" is the attempt to be faithful to the cathedral and earlier patterns of prayer, as distinct from the monastic pattern that is the dominant style of daily prayer in most other churches today.

Cathedral prayer was a rich service of praise and petition. Before the fourth century, an entire Christian community gathered both morning and evening for a brief, joyful service. Light was the dominant symbol. Led by clergy, yet emphasizing lay participation, the service, spoken in the people's native language, began with praise to God by using psalms (148–150 in the morning and 141 in the evening) and canticles (Scripture songs). Intercessions and petitions by the whole community followed the praise, and the intercessions and petitions ended with the Lord's Prayer. The service concluded with a blessing.

The role of Scripture in cathedral prayer was quite different from its role in modern United Methodist worship as most of us have known it. Cathedral prayer was not a service centered on preaching or teaching, nor was it an ascetic discipline. Scripture in cathedral prayer proclaimed God's redemptive grace in Christ.

The monastic prayer service was quite different. This pattern of prayer arose in monastic communities and urban centers where prayer became a whole way of life for especially earnest Christians. Instead of simply beginning and ending each day in prayer, these Christians took seriously the New Testament command to "pray without ceasing." In these communities, prayer was observed by the hours—sunrise, midmorning, noon, three, six, nine, midnight, and predawn. In these times of prayer, additional hymns, canticles, and the whole Psalter were sung. The role of Scripture changed. Increasingly, Scripture was read continuously and had a teaching role. The primary goal was to teach persons the whole Bible and promote their personal sanctification.

After Christianity became the official religion of the Roman Empire in the fourth century, and the Church consisted increasingly of persons converted by political or social pressure, whole communities no longer gathered for prayer. Increasingly, only the clergy and a few faithful laypersons continued to observe daily corporate prayer, and prayer services increasingly took on the monastic pattern. Prayer focused on personal rather than corporate spirituality. Corporate prayer shifted to the needs of monastic communities, not parish congregations.

As time passed, corporate prayer continued to evolve. As the monastic pattern of prayer prevailed, the laity participated less. The demands were too rigorous for persons in the secular world. When monks in A.D. 522/523 were required to say daily prayer in Latin, it signaled the beginning of the Middle Ages. Monastic communities themselves changed. As communities dispersed, daily prayer increasingly became a private, inward discipline of individuals and used less singing. This pattern continued through the next thousand years.

In 1549 the Church of England, which had recently declared its independence of the Pope, sought to restore daily corporate prayer to parish communities. Its *Book of Common Prayer* simplified the monastic prayer pattern into ascetic, non-ceremonial, and meditative services of "Morning Prayer" and "Evening Prayer." Scripture was read on a yearly cycle, and the whole Psalter was read monthly. The goal was to create a prayer pattern for the edification and instruction of clergy and laity.

This was the pattern John Wesley inherited two centuries later and adapted for use by the American Methodists in his *Sunday Service of the Methodists in North America* (1784).

In 1792, however, the American Methodists dropped these services of "Morning Prayer" and "Evening Prayer" as unsuited to their needs. Corporate weekday prayer among American Methodists, and also among Evangelicals and United Brethren, took such forms as midweek prayer meetings and prayer and praise services. They centered on hymn singing, extemporaneous prayer, and testimonies. In some segments of United Methodism these forms have retained their use and vigor; but in other sectors they have dropped away, leaving United Methodists without forms of corporate prayer other than the Sunday service.

In recent years there have been many attempts to revive corporate praise and prayer, and to discover practical patterns for such prayer. Particularly noteworthy has been the work of The Upper Room during the past fifty years. The Hymnal Revision Committee learned in the course of surveying United Methodists that there was a widespread desire that the new hymnal contain simple forms of corporate praise and prayer that could be used on any day of the week. Many persons and congregations were already interested in the classic forms of "Morning Prayer" and "Evening Prayer" and urged that these be adapted for the use of contemporary United Methodists. The Section on Worship of the General Board of Discipleship had already done some preliminary work in the area of daily prayer.

As a result, the Hymnal Revision Committee sought the help of the Section on Worship in developing "Orders of Daily Praise and Prayer." The Section, in consultation with the Hymnal Revision Committee, created a task force to develop a pattern of prayer for general use by United Methodists. The task force consulted with a wide range of United Methodists and with liturgical scholars of various denominations. A crucial decision was reached *not* to use the monastic prayer pattern but to develop orders that adapt the simple pattern of early Christian congregational praise and prayer to modern United Methodist use. The work of the task force was then presented, reviewed, revised, accepted by the Section on Worship and the Hymnal Revision Committee in May 1987, and adopted with one small amendment by General Conference in May 1988. These orders appear for the first time in this hymnal.

## C. CHARACTERISTICS OF THESE ORDERS

Both "Morning Praise and Prayer" and "Evening Praise and Prayer" share certain common characteristics. Several of these characteristics are held in common with similar services of other denominations, which are more influenced by monastic patterns. Other characteristics are distinctive to these particular services.

These services have as their basic goal what Robert Taft has described as the basic goal of Christian daily worship through the ages:

> A sanctification of life by turning to God at the beginning and end of each of its days to do what all liturgy always does—to celebrate and manifest in ritual moments what is and must be the constant stance of our every minute of the day: our unceasing priestly offering, in Christ, of self, to the praise and glory of the Father in thanks for [God's] saving gift in Christ.[12]

It is important to understand four of their characteristics.

1. Each service is Christ-centered. There is a constant focus in every act on the saving power of Jesus Christ. This focus on Christ puts everything in a new light. The rising of the sun and the lighting of an evening lamp or candle not only mark moments in daily life but also point toward the enduring presence of Jesus Christ in the community.

2. The fundamental pattern is that of praise followed by prayer. The title of each service indicates the twofold action: (a) praise for God's mighty acts and (b) the human response of prayer (intercession and petition). The decision to entitle these services "praise and prayer" rather than "prayer and praise" was intentional and carefully considered. In each service this pattern is more important than any particular act. This is the ancient and classic Christian pattern that grounds our prayer in what God has already done.

3. These services are intended for daily use. To be sure, few congregations or groups gather daily for prayer, except for limited periods of time as in conferences or evangelistic missions. But if every gathering of every group in a congregation prays together, and if praying individuals and families feel that their prayer is part of the corporate prayer of the congregation, daily corporate prayer becomes a reality that moves toward "ceaseless prayer" (I Thess. 5:17).

4. Each service is a community act of worship. These services are the work (liturgy) of all who gather. Leaders may or may not

---

12. Robert Taft, *The Liturgy of the Hours in East and West* (Collegeville, Minn.: Liturgical Press, 1986), pp. 359 ff.

be pastors. In many congregations lay leadership may be preferable and even essential. The rich inclusion of music throughout the service means that where possible it can be led by a company of singing voices. The use of inclusive language seeks to include the whole community in prayer.

## D. USING THESE ORDERS

These "Orders of Daily Praise and Prayer" may be used every time persons gather together in the name of Jesus Christ. As groups within your congregation begin and end their days in prayer, they will strengthen the Body of Christ.

Daily prayer can begin in the already existing gatherings of persons in your congregation. Rather than starting a special prayer group for the purpose of using these services, it may be better to encourage persons who already gather for the work of the church to use these orders. For example, encourage prayer in your Sunday school classes, Bible study groups, Youth Fellowship meetings, United Methodist Women and United Methodist Men meetings, Covenant Discipleship groups, neighborhood groups, shepherd groups, church staff meetings, church committee meetings, and family devotions. In each of these settings, enable persons to be intentional about a brief time of praise and prayer as they either begin the day or end the day. In many congregations, both small and large, this might mean almost immediately that at least once every day some members of the congregation are at prayer.

If each group is to be intentional about prayer, the congregation should be deliberate about training persons to lead prayer. For example, the pastor may dedicate part of an Administrative Council (or Administrative Board or Council on Ministries) meeting to train laypersons to lead such services. The focus should be on practical uses rather than on the historical and theological rationale for using these orders. Or, at a Council or Board retreat, train these leaders of the church to become the spiritual leaders of the congregation. And then encourage every meeting of the congregation to be a prayer group.

The setting for these services can be most helpful in making them effective. In general, people should be encouraged to pray where they gather rather than moving to some "sacred space." A classroom, meeting room, fellowship hall, garden, home, or apartment are appropriate locations for praise and prayer. A sanctuary or chapel may also be used, of course; but care should be exercised that this setting not make the services seem too formal and detract from the sense of community. Remember that the early Christians generally worshiped in houses rather than in church buildings as we know them. The goal should be to make praise and prayer fit into ordinary lives rather than being limited to holy places.

Seating should help create a sense of informal community. Have persons sit in some arrangement such as a circle where persons face one another. Here are several options (L = leader, D = desk for reading, C = candle or oil lamp for evening praise and prayer, † = cross):

The visible objects are signs pointing beyond themselves to spiritual reality. They are secondary yet important. They should be simple and unobtrusive, visible yet not dominating. A reading desk may be helpful, depending on the needs of the leader(s), but it is not necessary. A simple candle or oil lamp is a powerful sign of the light of Christ illumining the darkness, but if one is not available this should not prevent the holding of evening praise and prayer. An optional sign might be a basin of water at the doorway to help persons remember their baptism.

## E. MORNING PRAISE AND PRAYER

"Morning Praise and Prayer" begins the day with praise to God, followed by intercessory prayers. In so doing, it consecrates the day to God.

The primary sign is the rising sun. It is most effective if the service is held where natural sunlight can reach the room. As persons gather, greet one another in the name of Jesus Christ. The community may at this time indicate prayer concerns soon to be offered to God in the service—possibly by writing them on a sheet of paper posted on a wall or a table for that purpose.

## CALL TO PRAISE AND PRAYER

This may be divided between a leader and people or between two groups of people. It may be sung, using the following easily remembered tune:

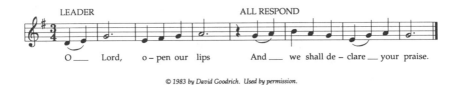

© 1983 by David Goodrich. Used by permission.

First Corinthians 15:57 may be used as an alternative call. It is appropriate to stand for this call and for the hymn that follows.

## MORNING HYMN

A hymn appropriate to the morning may be sung. If singing is not feasible it may be omitted, but even the smallest groups often find great blessing in singing. The "Index of Topics and Categories" (No. 947) in the hymnal lists appropriate hymns under the heading "Morning Prayer," but you are not limited to these particular hymns. Choose a hymn that is already known to the persons who have gathered; or, if you are introducing a new hymn, teach it to them before the service begins.

## PRAYER OF THANKSGIVING

This may be led by an individual or prayed in unison. The prayer printed at this point or some other prayer of thanksgiving may be used, or there may be spontaneous prayer of thanksgiving to God for the gift of Jesus Christ and for the day.

## [SCRIPTURE]

*Psalm 51 (No. 785), 63 (No. 788), or 95 (No. 814); Deuteronomy 6:4-7; Isaiah 55:1-3; John 1:1-5, 9-14; Romans 12:1-2; or other readings appropriate to the morning, or to the day or season of the Christian year, or to the nature of the occasion, may be used.*

## [SILENCE]

*Silent meditation on the scripture that has been read. This may be concluded with a short prayer.*

If the leader so chooses, there may be a Scripture reading followed by silent meditation at this point in the service. If these are included, the service takes on a partially reflective or "monastic" character, whereas if they are omitted the service has a more purely congregational ("cathedral") character.

The Scripture reading helps set the tone for the day and serves as the basis for silent reflection. Psalm 51 enables the community to confess their individual and corporate sin. Psalm 63 is a classic psalm for the morning. Psalm 95 is a psalm of praise appropriate for morning. Deuteronomy 6:4-9 is the Shema (see page 178). Isaiah 55:1-3 is a hymn of joy. John 1:1-5, 9-14 speaks of the light of the world. Romans 12:1-2 urges Christians to consecrate their lives to God. All these passages remind the community of God's grace. Other readings from Scripture may be appropriate, such as those that focus on the dawn, or reflect on the day or season of the Christian year or the work of that gathering or that day. A daily lectionary or other pattern of daily Bible reading may be used.

It is *not* intended that this Scripture reading be followed by preaching or spoken comments. This is a praise and prayer service, not a preaching service.

Silence is the natural response to this Scripture reading. During a time of silence of from one to three minutes, encourage persons to focus on the Scripture that has been read and apply it to their own lives. The leader may then end this time of silence with a brief, focused prayer such as: "God, accept our prayers in the name of your Son, Jesus Christ. **Amen.**"

## SONG OF PRAISE

*Psalm 100 (No. 821), 148 (No. 861), or 150 (No. 862); "Canticle of Zechariah" (No. 208); "Canticle of Moses and Miriam" (No. 135);*

*"Canticle of the Holy Trinity" (No. 80); "Canticle of God's Glory" (Nos. 82 and 83); "Canticle of Praise to God" (No. 91); "Canticle of Thanksgiving" (No. 74); "Canticle of Light and Darkness" (No. 205); or other Scripture song or hymn may be sung.*

This brings the opening "praise" half of the service to a strong climax. The classic patterns of daily worship have always encouraged Christians to praise God using words of Scripture. The Psalms have a special place as the chief "hymnal" of the Bible. Songs taken from other books of the Bible have traditionally been called "canticles." This recovery of Scripture song is a source of power and renewal for many Christian groups today.

Various possibilities are suggested here. Psalm 100, 148, or 150 may be read with or without the sung response. An alternative is to sing "All People That on Earth Do Dwell" (No. 75) or "Praise the Lord Who Reigns Above" (No. 96), which are paraphrases of Psalms 100 and 150 respectively. Other Scripture songs include "Canticle of Zechariah" (Luke 1:68-79, sometimes called the *Benedictus*), "Canticle of Moses and Miriam" (from Exod. 15), "Canticle of Praise to God" (taken from Pss. 95 and 96 and sometimes called the *Venite*), "Canticle of Thanksgiving" (Ps. 100 in the King James Version, sometimes called the *Jubilate*), and "Canticle of Light and Darkness" (selections from Isa. 9 and 59; Ps. 139; Dan. 2; I John 1). Two of the most ancient Christian hymns are also suggested here: "Canticle of the Holy Trinity" (the *Te Deum*, from the fourth century) and "Canticle of God's Glory" (the *Gloria in Excelsis* from the fourth-century church, which expands upon Luke 2:14). Each of these may be read with or without the sung response. Some other appropriate hymn of praise, especially one taken from Scripture, may also be sung.

## PRAYERS OF THE PEOPLE

*The following or other litany of intercession may be prayed, during which any person may offer a brief prayer of intercession or petition.*

*After each prayer, the leader may conclude:* "Lord, in your mercy," *and all may respond:* **"Hear our prayer."**

*Following these prayers, all may sing: "Hear Us, O God" (No. 490), "Jesus, Remember Me" (No. 488), "Let Us Pray to the Lord" (No. 485), "This Is Our Prayer" (No. 487), or "Remember Me" (No. 491).*

Here begins the second, or "prayer," half of the service, which is centered in a prayer or litany of intercession and petition.

The suggested pattern moves from the particular concerns of the gathered community to the cosmic cloud of witnesses. The leader begins: "Together, let us pray for the people of this congregation." Individuals then respond, speaking the name and needs of persons in that congregation. After each response is spoken, the leader prays: "Lord, in your mercy," and the people respond, **"Hear our prayer."** The leader then continues: "Let us pray for those who suffer and those in trouble." Again individuals respond; and after each response, the leader prays: "Lord, in your mercy," and the people respond, **"Hear our prayer."** Such prayers are then offered for the concerns of this local community, the world, the Church, and the communion of saints (including persons dead, alive, and yet to come).

There is a variety of alternatives. Either of the two litanies of intercession on pages 39-41 of *The Book of Services* may be used instead of the above pattern. "This Is Our Prayer" (487) or "Hear Us, O God" (490) may be the people's response after each petition. "Let Us Pray to the Lord" (485) may be used as the leader's and people's responses after each petition. If nothing that is suggested seems right for some particular group or situation, any other form or pattern of intercession may be used. What is most important is not some particular form or pattern but the reality of effective prayer.

In any event, a short sung response may be sung after the prayers as a whole. Among the possible responses are "Jesus, Remember Me" (485), which comes from France, and "Remember Me" (491), from the Black tradition.

THE LORD'S PRAYER

This sublime prayer may be spoken or sung (see 270, 271, 894-896). As the supreme Christian prayer, it is the climax of the "prayer" half of the service. By helping persons learn how to sing this prayer, leaders encourage persons to invest their whole selves in prayer. If instrumental accompaniment is required, it should be soft and not overwhelm the voices.

## BLESSING

The blessing is spoken by the leader to the people, facing them with eyes open. A variety of arm and hand gestures may be used in giving a blessing, but none of these is essential. The leader may use whatever gesture seems most natural or suitable to local custom, or omit gesture entirely. The blessing used here, often called the "Apostolic Blessing" (or "Apostolic Benediction"), is taken from II Corinthians 13:14. The people respond, **"Amen."**

## THE PEACE

*Signs of peace may be exchanged.*
What signs of peace are appropriate will vary from person to person and from group to group. A handclasp, a hug, words of blessing such as "The peace of Christ be with you this day," a single word such as "peace," are some of the signs that can be exchanged. No one should be made to feel uncomfortable or pressured to do something that does not come naturally.

The people then continue with the work of the day, knowing that the full day's tasks have been undergirded by praise and prayer.

## F. EVENING PRAISE AND PRAYER

"Evening Praise and Prayer" is traditionally associated with sunset as the time when a community ends its day or work together. Today that time may not literally be at sunset; it may be before or after sunset. This service might conclude an afternoon or all-day meeting. It might end the day on a church retreat. It might be a family's evening devotional, possibly centering around the dinner table. Most naturally, this service concludes a time together.

## PROCLAMATION OF THE LIGHT

*A candle may be lit and lifted in the midst of the community.*

An evening candle or lamp focuses attention on the light in the midst of darkness. Such a light should be large enough to be seen by all persons present. Other lights in the room may be turned down or off to increase this focus. The words of proclamation encourage the community to center on Jesus Christ. They may be sung, using the following easily remembered tune:

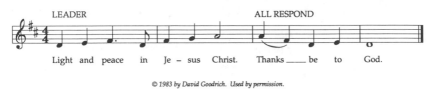

© 1983 by David Goodrich. Used by permission.

John 1:1-5 or Psalm 74:16 may be used as alternative words of proclamation.

## EVENING HYMN

*"O Gladsome Light" (No. 686) or other hymn appropriate to the evening may be sung.*

The ancient hymn "O Gladsome Light" is traditionally used at this point in the service. The "Index of Topics and Categories" in the hymnal lists appropriate hymns under the heading "Evening Prayer," but you are not limited to these particular hymns. Choose a hymn that is already known to those who have gathered; or, if you are introducing a new hymn, teach it to them before the service begins.

## PRAYER OF THANKSGIVING

This prayer may be led by an individual or prayed in unison. An alternative to the prayer printed in the hymnal is this adaptation of a prayer attributed to Bishop Hippolytus of the third century:

> We give you thanks, Almighty God,
>     through your Son Jesus Christ our Lord,
>     through whom you have shone upon us
>     and revealed to us the unfailing light.
> The daylight you created for our benefit
>     has satisfied us.
> We have completed the course of the day
>     and now come to the beginning of the night.
> Since now through your grace
>     we do not lack the light of evening,
> we praise and glorify you
>     through your Son Jesus Christ,
>     through whom be glory and power and honor to you
>     with the Holy Spirit,
>     both now and always and forever more.
> **Amen.**

Another prayer of thanksgiving may be used; or there may be informal, extemporaneous prayer of thanksgiving to God for the gift of Jesus Christ and for the day.

[SCRIPTURE]

> *Psalm 23 (Nos. 137 and 754), 90 (No. 809), 121 (No. 844), 141; Genesis 1:1-5, 14-19; Exodus 13:21-22; Matthew 25:1-13; Romans 5:6-11; I Thessalonians 5:2-10; Revelation 22:1-5; or other readings appropriate to the evening, or to the day or season of the Christian year, or to the nature of the occasion, may be used.*

[SILENCE]

> *Silent meditation on the scripture that has been read. This may be concluded with a short prayer.*

If the leader so chooses, there may be a Scripture reading followed by silent meditation at this point in the service. If these are included, the service takes on a partially reflective or "monastic" character, whereas if they are omitted the service has a more purely congregational ("cathedral") character.

The Scripture listed for this service guides the direction of this closing of the day. Psalm 23, the "shepherd psalm," offers hope in the midst of shadows. Psalm 90 affirms deliverance to an oppressed people. Psalm 121 encourages persons to ascend to God. Psalm 141:1-3 (not found in the hymnal) is an evening hymn of sacrifice, traditionally associated with the use of incense. Genesis 1:1-5, 14-19 reminds the community of God's good gift of creation. Exodus 13:21-22 describes how God guided the people through the dark wilderness. Matthew 25:1-13 carries an eschatological theme and encourages persons to watch for the Lord. Romans 5:6-11 urges a community to be reconciled one with another. First Thessalonians 5:1-10 also develops the theme of watchfulness. Revelation 22:1-5 promises life at the end of the age. Other Scripture may be chosen to reflect themes of light in the midst of darkness, to reflect the day or season of the Christian year, or to focus on the gathering just concluded.

As in "Morning Praise and Prayer," a short time of silence (one to three minutes), *not* a sermon or talk, follows. This may be concluded with a short, focused prayer, such as: "God, accept our prayers in the name of your Son, Jesus Christ. **Amen**."

## SONG OF PRAISE

> *Psalm 134 (No. 850), "Canticle of Mary" (No. 199), "Canticle of Simeon," (No. 225), "Canticle of Light and Darkness" (No. 205), "Canticle of Hope" (No. 734), and "Canticle of Covenant Faithfulness" (No. 125); or other Scripture song or hymn may be sung.*

This brings the opening "praise" half of the service to a strong climax. Psalm 134 may be read, sung, or read with the sung response as found in the hymnal. A further evening song of praise may follow Psalm 134 or replace it. "Canticle of Mary" (*Magnificat*, from Luke 1:46*b*-55), "Canticle of Simeon" (*Nunc Dimittis*, from Luke 2:29-32), "Canticle of Light and Darkness" (Isa. 9:2; 59:9-10; Ps. 139:11-12; Dan. 2:20, 22; I John 1:5), "Canticle of Hope" (Rev. 21:1-6, 23-24; 22:5, 12, 20), and "Canticle of Covenant Faithfulness" (Isa. 55:6-11) all may be sung, read responsively with sung responses, or read responsively. Each of these Scripture songs has a traditional use in evening prayer and helps lift up various themes for the community of faith. If none of these Scripture songs is used, another hymn or song of praise may be sung.

PRAYERS OF THE PEOPLE

> *The following or other litany of intercession may be prayed, during which any person may offer a brief prayer of intercession or petition. After each prayer, the leader may conclude:* Lord, in your mercy, *and all may respond:* **"Hear our prayer."**
>
> *Or, prayers of confession and words of pardon may be offered. See Nos. 890-893.*
>
> *Following these prayers, all may sing: "Hear Us, O God" (No. 490), "Lord, Have Mercy" (No. 482), "Kyrie Eleison" (Nos. 483, 484), or "Remember Me" (No. 491).*

Here begins the second, or "prayer," half of the service. A prayer or litany of intercession is the heart of this time of prayer. The same pattern is suggested here as was suggested for "Morning Praise and Prayer." The leader begins: "Together, let us pray for the people of this congregation." Individuals may then respond, speaking the name and needs of persons in that congregation. After each response is spoken, the leader prays, "Lord, in your mercy," and the people respond, **"Hear our prayer."** The leader then continues, "Let us pray for those who suffer and those in trouble." Again individuals respond; and after each response the leader prays, "Lord, in your mercy," and the people respond, **"Hear our prayer."** This pattern continues as prayers are then offered for the concerns of this local community, the world, the Church, and the communion of saints (including persons dead, alive, and yet to come).

If this pattern does not seem appropriate, there are alternatives. Either of the two litanies of intercession on pages 39-41 of *The Book of Services* may be used. "This Is Our Prayer" (487) or "Hear Us, O God" (490) may be the people's response to each petition. "Let Us Pray to the Lord" (485) may be used as the leader's and people's responses to each petition.

A prayer of confession and words of pardon are also appropriate. This may be spontaneous, or one of the confession-pardon sequences in the hymnal (890-893) may be used.

In any event, a short response such as "Hear Us, O God" (490); "Kyrie Eleison" (483, 484); "Jesus, Remember Me" (488); or "Remember Me" (491) may be sung at the close of this time of prayer, especially if it has included confession.

## THE LORD'S PRAYER

See comments on pages 189-90 above, under "Morning Praise and Prayer."

## BLESSING

The blessing is the last spoken act in the service. The service may then end in either of two distinctive ways. (1) The Peace may be shared by those present. This concludes the service on a joyful note. (2) Persons may leave in silence for a night of rest. This departure in silence gives a more meditative quality to the service. The last person to leave extinguishes the evening light.

Having thus concluded the day, the community may rest peacefully, aware of God's watchfulness over all creation.

## G. An Order of Praise and Prayer for Various Gatherings

There are many occasions in the life of any congregation when persons gather for prayer other than in the morning or evening. When a group wishes to end its morning work, or to offer prayer at noon or in the afternoon, or to begin an evening with prayer, something other than "Morning Praise and Prayer" or "Evening Praise and Prayer" may be appropriate.

An order for such a service, entitled "An Order of Praise and Prayer for Various Gatherings," was originally to be in the hymnal; but there was not room for it. It is printed here, with commentary, for those who may find it useful.

Flexibility is the strength of this order. It offers numerous possibilities for every act of worship. It also demands, however, that leaders be intentional as they plan. The following comments suggest only a few of the possible ways to use this order.

## CALL TO PRAISE AND PRAYER

*Brief invitations to praise and prayer or scripture sentences may be offered.*

This may be a short biblical or other invitation to the community to enter into a time of praise and prayer. Scripture sentences might include: Psalm 118:24 or 124:8; Isaiah 40:30-31; Lamentations 3:25-26; John 4:23-24, or Romans 6:4. They may be chosen to fit the time of day or the nature of the gathering—for example, "May the Lord bless us as we gather for this midday meal."

## HYMN

*A hymn appropriate to the time of day, or to the day or season of the Christian year, or to the nature of the occasion, may be sung.*

## PRAYER OF THANKSGIVING

This may be a general prayer of thanksgiving or one that focuses on particular blessings related to the occasion.

## [SCRIPTURE]

*One or more readings, appropriate to the time of day, or to the day or season of the Christian year, or to the nature of the occasion, may be used.*

## [SILENCE]

*Silent meditation on the Scripture that has been read. This may be concluded with a short prayer.*

If the leader so chooses, there may be a Scripture reading followed by silent meditation at this point in the service. See the comments on pages 187 and 192 under "Morning and Evening Praise and Prayer."

## SONG OF PRAISE

*Here is sung or said one or more of the following: "Canticle of the Holy Trinity" (No. 80), "Canticle of Moses and Miriam" (No. 135),*

*"Canticle of Hope" (No. 734), or other psalm of praise, Scripture song, or hymn.*

This is the climax of the "praise" half of the service. The "Canticle of the Holy Trinity" (the *Te Deum*, the fourth century), "Canticle of Moses and Miriam" (from Exodus 15), and "Canticle of Hope" (from Rev. 21; 22) are appropriate on any occasion. Psalms 113, 121, 122, 124, and 126 are appropriate for midday prayer. Psalms 4, 33, 34, 91, 134, and 139:1-12 are appropriate for night prayer.

## PRAYERS OF THE PEOPLE

*A litany of intercession and petition may be prayed, during which any person may offer a brief prayer of intercession or petition. After each prayer, the leader may conclude:* "Lord, in your mercy," *and all may respond:* **"Hear our prayer."**
*Or, prayers for the day, season, or gathering may be offered.*
*Or, prayers for healing may be offered, such as the prayer "For the Sick" (457).*

Here begins the "prayer" half of the service. Again, intercessory prayer is the heart of this act of worship. Encourage every person to lift up prayer concerns, which may include petitions for individuals, situations, and communities, as well as for the world and Church. Spontaneity and openness should be encouraged. This time of prayer may conclude with a collect or other short, focused prayer appropriate to the day, season of the Christian year, or nature of the gathering.

Prayers for healing may be appropriate, either with or without the laying on of hands or anointing with oil. They may also be appropriate in either "Morning Praise and Prayer" or "Evening Praise and Prayer," or at a Service of Word and Table.

## THE LORD'S PRAYER

*Sung or spoken. See Nos. 270, 271, 894-896.*
See comment on page 189 under "Morning Praise and Prayer."

BLESSING

*A blessing may be given. Signs of peace may be exchanged.*
The blessing may be as simple as, "To God be honor and glory forever and ever" (I Tim. 1:17b).
Exchanging the peace is optional.

## H. CONCLUSION

These "Orders of Daily Praise and Prayer" are now offered to our church. May their use enable United Methodists to sing praises and offer prayers to God. Thus, may we be renewed as the body of Christ every day.

# CHAPTER 11

# ACTS OF WORSHIP

## A. AFFIRMATIONS OF FAITH

### THE NICENE CREED (880)

This creed is the most universally used creed in Christendom. It is a revision by the Council of Constantinople in 381 of the creed drawn up by the Council of Nicea in 325. Wesley used this creed when he used *The Book of Common Prayer* but did not include it in *The Sunday Service of the Methodists in North America* (1784). Its first use in American Methodism was in *The Book of Worship* (1965) and *The Book of Hymns* (1966). It is a powerful symbol and affirmation of our unity with other Christian churches. The English translation here is the most ecumenical one available—that of the International Consultation on English Texts (1975), as revised in 1987 by its successor the English Language Liturgical Commission.

### THE APOSTLES' CREED, TRADITIONAL VERSION (881)

This is the creed most familiar to United Methodists, many of whom know it by heart. It was used at baptisms by the church at Rome at the beginning of the third century. Because it is the traditional baptismal creed both of Roman Catholics and Protestants, it is both a statement of the faith of the ecumenical Church and a reminder of the covenant into which we have been baptized.

The phrase "He descended into hell" has traditionally been included in the creed and was retained by Wesley. It was omitted in the 1905 and 1935 Methodist hymnals and the 1957

EUB hymnal. It was included as a footnote in the 1966 *Methodist Hymnal*, and that footnote is retained in this hymnal. The phrase in the original Latin *(descendit ad inferna)* literally means "he went down to the lower regions" and does not necessarily refer to the realm of eternal punishment. It underscores the assertion of Jesus' death in the previous line. It may also refer to the teaching in I Peter 3:18-20 that Christ was "put to death in the flesh but made alive in the spirit, in which he went and preached to the spirits in prison, who formerly did not obey." It may also refer to Christ's going to do battle with Satan for the deliverance of the saints. It might better be translated, "He descended to the dead."

The word "catholic" means simply "universal" and does not refer in particular to the Roman Catholic Church. In an amendment to the hymnal report, the General Conference voted to include a footnote explaining this wherever the Apostles' Creed occurs in the hymnal.

## THE APOSTLES' CREED, ECUMENICAL VERSION (882)

This is the ecumenically accepted modern translation of the Apostles' Creed, that of the International Consultation on English Texts (1975), with several revisions made in 1987 by its successor the English Language Liturgical Commission.

The phrase "He descended to the dead" clarifies the meaning of the phrase formerly translated "He descended into hell." See the explanation of this phrase in the Apostles' Creed, Traditional Version.

## A STATEMENT OF FAITH OF THE UNITED CHURCH OF CANADA (883)

This contemporary statement of faith was drawn up and officially adopted by the United Church of Canada. It has been widely used by United Methodists since a previous version of it was included in *The Sacrament of the Lord's Supper: An Alternate Text 1972*.

## THE STATEMENT OF FAITH OF THE KOREAN METHODIST CHURCH (884)

This statement of faith was drawn up and officially adopted by the Korean Methodist Church when it was organized in 1930.

An English translation of it appeared in the 1935 and 1966 Methodist hymnals and has been widely used by American United Methodists. When it was being considered for inclusion in the new hymnal, Korean American United Methodists pointed out that certain parts of the existing English translation do not adequately translate the original Korean. Dal Joon Wan and Sang E. Chun then did retranslations from the Korean and proposed the revisions that have now been incorporated into the text.

## A MODERN AFFIRMATION (885)

This affirmation is well known to United Methodists because of its inclusion in the 1935 and 1966 editions of *The Methodist Hymnal*. It first appeared in 1932 in the *Book of Service* containing the Ritual and orders of worship that had just been adopted by the Methodist Episcopal Church and in the *Book of Common Worship for Use in the Several Communions of the Church of Christ*, co-edited by Bishop Wilbur P. Thirkfield of the Methodist Episcopal Church and Dr. Oliver Huckel, pastor of the Congregational Church, Greenwich, Connecticut. Bishop Thirkfield had chaired the commission that had prepared the 1932 revision of the Methodist Episcopal Ritual and also chaired the Commission on Worship of the Federal Council of Churches, predecessor of the National Council of Churches. It is not known who wrote the preface spoken by the pastor alone, but the affirmation itself was written by Professor Edwin Lewis, distinguished Methodist theologian at Drew University, at the request of Bishop Thirkfield.

## THE WORLD METHODIST SOCIAL AFFIRMATION (886)

This affirmation was adopted by the World Methodist Council when it met at Nairobi, Kenya, in 1986. It had been drawn up by the Council's Social and International Affairs Committee in a process that included the following: (a) all member denominations were invited to send a copy of their current statement of social principles; (b) representatives of each region of world Methodism met for a week and after intensive Bible study and examination of all the social principles statements formulated a first draft; (c) this draft was sent back to the member denominations for their response; and (d) the responses received were the basis of revisions in preparing the final draft for submission to the World Methodist Council, from which the hymnal version was drawn.

## AFFIRMATION FROM ROMANS 8:35, 37-39 (887)

Paul's conviction that nothing can separate us from God's love is particularly pertinent on occasions when such separation may appear to exist. While this affirmation can be used for general purposes, it is especially appropriate for funerals and memorial services or in times of disaster and distress.

For congregational use, the Pauline affirmation "I am sure" has been changed to "we are sure." "Through him who loved us" has been changed to "through the One who loved us" to make the reading more inclusive. Apart from these changes, the affirmation follows the Revised Standard Version.

## AFFIRMATION FROM I CORINTHIANS 15:1-6 AND COLOSSIANS 1:15-20 (888)

This affirmation focuses upon the person and the saving work of Jesus Christ. Language is inclusive, both for humanity and for Christ.

The leader's part and the opening paragraph for the people is an edited form of I Corinthians 15:1-6. Paul's references to himself have been deleted; and in accordance with the reports of the Gospels, the fact that the risen Lord appeared first to the women has been added.

The second paragraph of the people's part draws its content from Colossians 1:15-20, in a form designed for ease for pubic reading and understanding.

This affirmation may be used on any Sunday, since each Lord's Day is a joyful commemoration of the resurrection; but it is particularly appropriate throughout the Great Fifty Days from Easter through Pentecost.

## AFFIRMATION FROM I TIMOTHY 2:5-6; 1:15; 3:16 (889)

There is embedded in I Timothy 3:16 a statement that may have had creedal status in the New Testament church even before the writing of First Timothy. Thus the author may be quoting a statement of faith already known to the readers of the letter. This statement here is introduced by other passages from the same New Testament book, to provide a full congregational affirmation, but one marked by brevity and inclusive language.

The statement proclaims both the earthly work of Jesus and the transcendent dimensions of Christ's glory and reign. It is suitable for use whenever a concise statement in biblical language is desired.

## CONFESSION, ASSURANCE, AND PARDON

890. This contemporary confession and pardon is from *The Book of Common Prayer (1979)*.

891. This traditional confession from the service of "Morning Prayer" in *The Book of Common Prayer* was included in the *Sunday Service*, which Wesley sent to the Methodists in America. It has been much used by United Methodists, having been included in the 1935 and 1966 Methodist hymnals and the 1957 EUB hymnal.

The words of assurance are from I John 1:9. It is appropriate that the people respond, "Thanks be to God."

892. This confession was introduced to Methodists in an order of worship adopted by the 1932 Methodist Episcopal General Conference and then in the 1935 hymnal. It has been widely used ever since.

The words of assurance are from I Timothy 1:15 and I John 2:1-2. It is appropriate that the people respond, "Thanks be to God."

893. This contemporary litany of confession comes from the Cathedral Church of Saint George in Cape Town, South Africa, which is currently Archbishop Desmond Tutu's cathedral.

Any of these prayers of confession may be introduced by a call to confession, such as one of the following:
1. Christ our Lord calls all who love him
earnestly to repent of their sin
and live in peace with one another.
Therefore, let us confess our sin
before God and one another.
*(The Book of Services)*

2. Let us confess our sins against God and our neighbor.
*(The Book of Common Prayer)*
3. Let us humbly confess our sins unto Almighty God.
*(The Book of Common Prayer)*

## C. THE LORD'S PRAYER

ECUMENICAL TEXT (894)

This 1975 translation by the International Consultation on English Texts was a response to the widely expressed need for a common, ecumenical translation of the Lord's Prayer for English-speaking Christians. Since that time this text has been widely adopted in the hymn and prayer books of English-speaking Christian denominations throughout the world.

It meets a special need of United Methodists, since Methodists and Evangelical United Brethren used different translations of the Lord's Prayer. Many persons at the time of the 1968 union that produced The United Methodist Church expressed the hope that, instead of using the word "trespasses" (Methodist) or "debts" (EUB), we would use the word "sins" as a symbol of our unity. Also, "sins" expresses most plainly what is meant by the less direct words "trespasses" and "debts."

*Prayers We Have in Common* (1975), which contains the ICET texts with the translators' commentary, has this to say about the phrase, "Save us from the time of trial":

> Two errors must be avoided in this line: the first is the misconception that God can be the agent of temptation, and the second is that the original Greek word means "temptation" as it is meant today. The reference here is primarily eschatological. It is probably a petition for deliverance from the final "time of trial" which, in biblical thought, marks the Last Days and the full revelation of anti-Christ. The peril envisaged is that of apostasy— the renunciation of the Christian faith in the face of the suffering and persecution which is expected to herald the final triumph of God's Kingdom (Luke 23:31, 32, 40; Revelation 3:10). Yet a reference to any occasion of testing, when issues of life and death are in the balance, is not excluded. Either way, it is certainly not subjective moral

temptations that are basically envisaged. The suggested translation seems to be the most adequate available.[13]

## FROM THE RITUAL OF THE METHODIST CHURCH (895)

This translation, used in the Ritual of the former Methodist Church and most familiar to former Methodists, came originally from *The Book of Common Prayer* (1549). A few alterations have been made in the intervening centuries, chiefly the addition of the final doxology, "For thine is the kingdom . . . ," in 1662.

## FROM THE RITUAL OF THE
## EVANGELICAL UNITED BRETHREN CHURCH (896)

This translation, used in the Ritual of the former Evangelical United Brethren Church, comes, with minor alterations, from the King James Version of the Bible (Matt. 6:9-13). It is most familiar, not only among former Evangelical United Brethren, but among those Protestants who have no prayerbook tradition and have taken the Lord's Prayer directly from the Bible.

---

13. *Prayers We Have in Common*, 2nd rev. ed. (Philadelphia: Fortress Press, 1975), p. 3.

# BIBLIOGRAPHY

*Companion to The Book of Services.* Nashville: Abingdon Press, 1988. A full account of the story and theological rationale of the new services.

*Holy Communion.* Nashville: Abingdon Press, 1987. A book of communion resources for use by the pastor, in planning and while conducting services at the Lord's table.

*The Book of Services.* Nashville: United Methodist Publishing House, 1985. Contains the new official Ritual adopted by the 1984 General Conference and included in the new hymnal. Leatherette pocket edition is especially useful for the pastor to carry when bringing communion to the sick and shut-in, at funerals, and on other occasions where the convenience of a pocket book of ritual is important.

*The Hymns of the United Methodist Hymnal.* Sanchez, Diana vol. ed. Nashville: Abingdon Press, 1989. The companion to this volume, giving stories and practical helps for using each of the hymns, canticles, and interspersed acts of worship in the new hymnal.

*The United Methodist Worship Planning Calendar.* Published annually by The United Methodist Publishing House, with lectionary readings, suggested colors, hymn suggestions, and planning space for each Sunday.

Davies, J. G., ed. *The New Westminster Dictionary of Liturgy and Worship.* Philadelphia: Westminster Press, 1986. A one-volume encyclopedia of information about worship history and practices throughout the world.

Garcia, Barbara (ed.). *God's Children in Worship* (multi-media kit). Nashville: Discipleship Resources, 1988. A study of worship for children, parents, and congregations.

Garcia, Barbara, and Kriewald, Diedra. *The Communion Book for Children.* Nashville: Discipleship Resources, 1984. For use by children during the service, in church school, or at home.

Garcia, Barbara. *Worship: Images Involving Children* (video cassette). Nashville: Discipleship Resources, 1988. Deals with children's participation in corporate worship.

Hickman, Hoyt L. *A Primer for Church Worship.* Nashville: Abingdon Press, 1984. An introduction to worship for both pastors and laypersons.

Hickman, Hoyt L. (ed.); Sallers, Don E.; Stookey, Laurence Hull; White, James F. *Handbook of the Christian Year.* Nashville: Abingdon Press, 1986. A comprehensive resource for understanding and observing the Christian year. Contains acts and services of worship for each of the days and seasons of the Christian year, including the entire three-year Common Lectionary.

Hickman, Hoyt L. *Planning Worship Each Week.* Nashville: Discipleship Resources, 1988. A practical guide for planning services week by week.

Hickman, Hoyt L. *United Methodist Altars.* Nashville: Abingdon Press, 1984. A practical guide to planning the environment of worship.

Hickman, Hoyt L. *The Acolyte's Book.* Nashville: Abingdon Press, 1985. A training booklet for use with acolytes.

Johnson, Kenneth M. *Ushering and Greeting.* Nashville: Discipleship Resources, 1989. A practical guide for church ushers and greeters.

Langford, Thomas A., III, *Your Ministry of Planning a Christian Funeral.* Nashville: Discipleship Resources, 1989. A booklet to use in planning funerals.

Langford, Thomas A., III and Bonnie Jones Gehweiler, *The Worship Handbook.* Nashville: Discipleship Resources, 1984. A practical and comprehensive guide for leaders of worship.

Langford, Thomas A., III, and Langford, Sally Overby. *Worship and Evangelism.* Nashville: Discipleship Resources, 1989. Discusses the mutually supportive relationship of worship and evangelism.

Snow, M. Lawrence. *Planning a Christian Wedding.* Nashville: Discipleship Resources, 1988. A booklet to use with couples in planning their wedding.

Stookey, Laurence Hull. *Baptism: Christ's Act in the Church.* Nashville: Abingdon Press, 1982. A theology of Baptism.

Ward, Richard. *Reading Scripture Aloud.* Nashville: Discipleship Resources, 1989. Practical helps for those who read Scripture in worship.

White, James F. and Susan J. *Church Architecture: Building and Renovating for Christian Worship.* Nashville: Abingdon Press, 1988. A comprehensive and practical guide for designing or renovating sanctuaries or chapels.

White, James F. *Introduction to Christian Worship.* Nashville: Abingdon Press, 1980. A basic seminary textbook on worship.

Willimon, William H. *Remember Who You Are.* Nashville: The Upper Room, 1980. A basic study book on Baptism for laypersons.

Willimon, William H. *Sunday Dinner.* Nashville: The Upper Room, 1981. A basic study book on Holy Communion for laypersons.

Willimon, William H. *With Glad and Generous Hearts.* Nashville: The Upper Room, 1986. A basic study book on Sunday worship for laypersons.

Willimon, William H. *Your Child Is Baptized.* (Revised Edition) Nashville: Discipleship Resources, 1989. A booklet for parents whose child has just been baptized.